GOOD MUSLIM BOY

OSAMAH SAMI

hardie grant books
MELBOURNE · LONDON

Published in 2015 by Hardie Grant Books

Hardie Grant Books (Australia)
Ground Floor, Building 1
658 Church Street
Richmond, Victoria 3121
www.hardiegrant.com.au

Hardie Grant Books (UK)
5th & 6th Floor
52–54 Southwark Street
London SE1 1UN
www.hardiegrant.co.uk

All rights reserved. No part of this publication may be reproduced, stored in a retrieval system or transmitted in any form by any means, electronic, mechanical, photocopying, recording or otherwise, without the prior written permission of the publishers and copyright holders.

The moral rights of the author have been asserted.
Copyright text © Osamah Sami, 2015

A Cataloguing-in-Publication entry is available from the catalogue of the National Library of Australia at www.nla.gov.au
Good Muslim Boy
ISBN 978 1 74270 615 3

Cover design by Mark Campbell
Weaving by Cathy Tipping
Text design by Patrick Cannon
Typeset in 11.5/16 pt Berkeley Oldstyle by Cannon Typesetting

Printed in Australia by Griffin Press

The paper this book is printed on is certified against the Forest Stewardship Council® Standards. Griffin Press holds FSC chain of custody certification SGS-COC-005088. FSC promotes environmentally responsible, socially beneficial and economically viable management of the world's forests.

Contents

Foreword by Andrew Knight	vi
Prologue	ix
Mortar melodies	1
The day God died	14
A merciless magic	28
The tall male was of excellent hygiene	36
Cheeky son of a cleric man	41
Sipping tea with sugar	59
Girls, girls, girls	67
We'll get there when we get there	83
The great escape	89
Thank you for your cooperation	98
Culture shock	104
Sleeping rough	120
Lessons to learn	127
Paperwork is paperwork	149
Truth isn't the best medicine	163
Inshallah	174
Faking it	180
Market trading	196
Stolen dreams	207
Clearance	227
Repentance	237
Man of a thousand senses	252

For my father—
my confidant, friend and absolute hero

FOREWORD

By Andrew Knight

I first met Osamah at filmmaker Tony Ayres's home in Elwood. Tony had approached me to co-write a film with a first time writer, the son of the head cleric of Melbourne's Shiite community. On the short walk to Tony's house I was rehearsing the many ways I could politely say, 'Get me out of this'. Tony and I often talked about working on something, but a political tract on the complexities of Islamic life in Melbourne seemed a bridge too far.

Also, the fact that it meant working with a first time writer for whom English wasn't his first language didn't exactly thrill me. But this was a time when this country's abuse of refugees and the growing fear campaign was reaching its now-permanent crescendo—so I saw some merit in at least having the chat. On the phone I had pushed Tony on the theme. He duck-fudged a bit before admitting it really wasn't that kind of story. 'It's more—it's a…well, it's a kind of fucked-up romantic comedy about a…it's…can you just meet this guy? You'll really like him, he's super talented and he's very good looking.'

FOREWORD

So I found myself sitting in Tony and Michael's living room with its alarming crack in the wall (then more window than crack) talking to this…yes, annoyingly good-looking man. Six hours later I left not only agreeing to do the movie, but believing I had just collided with one of the most gifted young people I have ever met.

What do you need to know about Osamah—he of the unfortunate first name? He is a lousy Muslim. He tries hard. He is committed to his faith and loves its central teachings and rituals, but man does he wrestle with it. His private life is always in chaos and deeply amusing to observe. You find yourself laughing at him as much as with him. He speaks with a first generation Australian twang that disguises the fact he speaks six other languages. In the time we worked together, he taught himself near-perfect French on the internet and has probably added another tongue since last we spoke a few weeks ago. He is a genuine polymath with a formidable intellect. He reads far and wide. He is a great sportsman—though I only have his word for this. He thankfully barracks, loudly, for Essendon and holds a 1st Dan black belt in karate. He plays cricket and football and builds and plays ouds and several other instruments. He does fine calligraphy, can fix my computer, never pays a parking fine and as a result is always in some pointless dispute with authority. He has a great and compassionate heart, an unquenchable enthusiasm for life, great humour, two children and, oh, he can act—very well as it happens—and for someone for whom English is only his third (or is it fourth?) language, he writes beautifully.

This book chronicles some of the least sane periods in Osamah's already insane life; the fact that these events are true beggars belief. This book will delight the reader.

We need someone in the world to be our yardstick, a benchmark by which we may assess our own gaffs and shortcomings. Osamah is our man.

His writing affords a reader a genuinely warm and hysterical insight into an Islamic community struggling to make sense of and fit into a purportedly liberal, secular Australia. That tussle provides endless material for this writer.

As Osamah's mother says in our script: 'The Koran was written before this country was discovered—the Prophet never saw Australian beaches.' Being with Osamah, reading his words, you can not help but gain some appreciation of this singular, largely Arabic world secreted in our inner suburbs. You grow to love these people—as wonderful, flawed and crazy as the rest of us. In that sense, perhaps Osamah's writing is more seductively political and life affirming than any trenchant criticism.

Andrew Knight 19.04.15

PROLOGUE

Melbourne, Australia, 2013

When you've grown up the way I did, an *Iraqi* boy born in *Iran* while the two countries were at war, you think there's not much left that can scare you.

And yet, here we were, gathered in the house behind the mosque in Melbourne, where my father, the cleric, had summoned me, an adult man, away from my own wife and daughter, almost like I was seven years old again. Almost like back in Iran.

He wore a familiar facial expression: absolute benevolence tossed with a natural flair for absolute ass-kicking justice.

'So a caravan of elders came to the mosque today,' he breezily said. 'They demanded I disown you. Even better, they demanded I send you to Iran so that you could face the death penalty.' He smiled.

I remained silent and flicked through the index of crimes that might have upset the community. Was it my marriage? My work? My education? Something I'd done long ago, in the past?

My father put me out of my misery. 'Son, it's about YouTube,' he said.

I face-palmed. I knew what he meant.

The son of the cleric had appeared in a gay movie on the internet.

My relationship with the community was already under strain—as it had been my whole life to this point, for a variety of colourful reasons. Lately, all these reasons had had to do with my acting career. I'd appeared opposite Claudia Karvan as a refugee who slept with a married woman (Community Outrage O'Meter: eight). I'd most recently displeased them by playing a Lebanese man engaged to a lesbian (that was a nine).

Playing a gay man—well, we needed the Richter scale for that one. It was one giant earthquake that would leave aftershock after tremor after aftershock for a long time yet. But this hadn't been a high-profile role, the kind the community would notice. It had been a small role in a short film project, filmed years ago.

In retrospect, I probably should've predicted that a community member would somehow manage to stumble upon a gay flick on YouTube. It was remarkable how often our nosy neighbours would 'accidentally' dig up evidence of my sins in exactly this fashion. Of course, once they'd seen it, what could they do but send a mass email blast to hundreds of local Iraqis? Every Iraqi with bluetooth enabled had a chance to freeze-frame the exact moment I embraced a—gasp—white man—double gasp—bare-chested.

I'd had a long time to make my peace with the judgement of our community. But the problem with a small immigrant community was you were never quite a lone ranger. For every casually abusive comment I'd get, thanks to my Western behaviour, Dad always received ten times the letters, ten times the questions.

PROLOGUE

His role as the visionary local imam was coveted by a handful of hopeful aspirants. Every wrong step I took was exactly the ammo they needed against Dad.

'I think we should get out of this place and have you blow off some meaningful steam,' Dad suggested.

My wife was interstate at the time; Dad pronounced, 'So let her be. Bring your daughter, your mother will look after her. We'll go away for a few weeks, get you freshened up, and come back with a new perspective.'

He grinned at me while sipping his pineapple juice. This suggested he'd planned a holiday somewhere tropical: maybe Hawaii or Bermuda. None of this was plausible when we were talking about my dad.

Still, he went on. 'It's important to connect with yourself before you can recharge,' he said.

He was speaking slowly, naturally having a conversation with himself out loud, convincing himself this would be a good idea, exactly what he and I needed.

'I'm not saying the change of scenery alone will change your state of mind. For if inside you are trapped, you will always remain trapped. No matter where you are. Even on the moon!

'But these experiences will change you. I'm sure you'll do amazing things and come back, I dare say, a different man.'

I nodded in tentative agreement.

'I just want you to know, Osamah, that, as always, there is no judgement on my end on any aspect of your life, even the parts of it which I am sure you personally regret.'

He set down his pineapple juice and dusted his hands, clearly wrapping up the conversation.

'So, we will go together and God willing have a great time.'

He finished with an enormous, fatherly smile.

Well, so far, so good, I thought. *Free holiday with Dad.*

'You're right,' I said. 'I need a new wave of energy to wash my mind and body clean. And what better way than a trip with a man I admire and love?'

We smiled at each other. This would be good.

'And Iran is beautiful this time of year,' he said.

My stomach dropped a hundred kilometres. 'Iran?' I swallowed a hot ball of saliva.

If I'd known what the trip would really be like, I would've thrown up all over the carpet.

MORTAR MELODIES

Abadan City, Iran, 1988

The six-year-old man of the house

I was a child in unfortunate circumstances.

It was a freezing winter in late '80s Iran, right on the Iraqi border. Anywhere there was oil, there was turmoil—so Dad liked to say—and in Abadan, oil was produced faster than on a teenager's face. My city of Abadan had been swapping flags with Iraq since the war began. One day it was theirs; the next it was ours. I didn't even know who *we* or *they*—*us* or *them*—were, and I don't know now, either. I'm an Iraqi by heritage who was born in Iran, so I've always been at war with myself.

The Iraq–Iran War had started eight years before for the same reason as most other wars: no reason, or at least none I could fathom. All I knew was the Ayatollah of Iran and Saddam Hussein of Iraq didn't exactly want to sit down and settle this with some homemade lemonade and a game of Monopoly—which was probably for the best, given how people sometimes feel about each other after they play Monopoly.

These days Abadan belonged to Iran, so the green, red and white flag was proudly anchored on every building in town except ours. Dad was an Iraqi, therefore I was an Arab, therefore the neighbourhood hated us. I couldn't even say hello to the five-year-old Persian girl across the road. Our apartment block, mainly peopled with Iraqis like ourselves, flew our flaccid 'peace flag' from a drainpipe on the rooftop. We couldn't raise the Iraqi flag—that would constitute treason. Nor did we have the heart to put up the Iranian flag, so we made a peace flag from our overused white *dishdashas* (long Arab dresses) and solemnly displayed our wish to end the brutal years.

Our place was a tiny, one-bedroom, women-filled space—some boys, but we were severely outnumbered. There was Mum, two aunts, two wives of uncles, Grandma and ten little girls. By the time I was six, I was the man of the house. My brother Mohammed, aka Moe Greene, was four, my other brother was in nappies and, apart from my two young cousins, all the other men were on the front line.

We lived here because we were a tight family unit—or that's what we were told to tell the neighbours. Truth is, we couldn't afford anything bigger.

Only the bedrooms had mattresses, and although they were thin, they were still better than sleeping in the hallway, where we rolled our blankets on top of us to sleep in a cocoon. Five metres, a dozen people, all side by side, waiting to rotate into the bedroom. We split up time on those three mattresses as fairly as we could. Every six days it was my turn; the rest of the time, my back really ached for it.

In such a situation, aside from an exit strategy to get to the bunkers during an air raid, the issue of utmost importance was maintaining your oral hygiene. In the hallway, you could always smell five breaths at the same time: a cocktail of toothpaste, the acids you get in empty guts and general dental wear and tear. Some days, my cousins and I played games of breath-volleyball: we tried to lob rancid breath into each other's nostrils, a deep, rounded gust of rotten air directly up the nose of your opponent. If your opponent acknowledged the rotten breath and screamed—'Pwaaahhh!'—you scored a point.

There was a strict one-minute limit on the showers. Shampoo: ten seconds; wash face: ten seconds; wash body: twenty seconds. If you got this right, you had a cool twenty seconds of luxury left to do as you pleased. Sing folklore songs, dream of escaping the war…anything. But if you didn't wake up at 5 am, forget it—even the cold water ran out, under daily restrictions.

Also, everyone yelled that their shit didn't stink; it had to be the person before them. I was amazed at how much of a stink the girls could make. I'd always thought girls took more feminine shits, but they could really outdo the boys in that department.

Therapy from a fortune teller

So my dad, the Iraqi, was fighting for the Iranians—but his brothers, my uncles, fought for Iraq.

Like any six-year-old, I had a galaxy of questions.

'Mum.'

'Yes, *sowmeh* love.' (She called me *sowmeh* when I was in her good books. Otherwise, it was 'you little son of a shit', or 'you two-legged goat', which was her classic.)

'Iran is the good side.'

'Yes, you know this, *sowmeh*.'

'And the people who fight them are evil. How evil?'

'Enough that they'll all go to hell.'

'All of them?'

'Yes, dear. Regardless. Stop asking these questions.'

'But the good people, they go to heaven. Right?'

'Yes. We call them martyrs.'

'So. If Dad died in the war, he'd be a martyr.'

'*Sowmeh!* That's your father you're talking about.'

'Don't you always say heaven is a good place? Why wouldn't you want Dad to go there?'

'We don't want your dad killed. You should be praying for him.'

'I always pray.'

'Good boy.'

'I have one last question.'

Mum let out a bowl's worth of air. 'You're getting on my nerves,' she said, palms widening, ready for a smack.

'Why do my uncles fight for the evil side?'

'That's a question for grown-ups, *sowmeh*.'

When I thought this through at bedtime, it was increasingly confusing. I wanted to pray for Dad to stay alive; I also wanted to pray for his brothers. And because I knew they were evil, and that they didn't deserve my prayers, I wondered if this made me a bad person.

I looked up at my mum. She was a very young woman, about twenty-two. She was staring into nowhere. I got upset. I didn't want her to cry. Most of my questions led to this scenario.

Eventually, in lieu of having the appropriate answers, she took me to see a specialist. Or, her version of a specialist: a fortune teller.

The fortune teller was old. Like, really, really old. My point of reference for an old person was Noah, who'd lived to a thousand; I was pretty sure this woman was older.

Her hands freaked me out while she examined my palm. It was like death and history and ghosts and shedding skin were all touching my flesh at once.

She looked at me with her one green eye—the other looked like one of those tunnels that they blow through the mountains using dynamite. She paused for an entire minute and then revealed her prophecy: 'Osamah, when you grow up, you're going to become a therapist.'

Mum's response was whip-quick. 'You mean he'll *need* a therapist when he grows up. For a long, long time.' She took my hand and stormed out of the small, smelly tent. I remember her hands—so soft after the fortune teller's, like winter turned to spring. I had never in my life felt more comforted.

Not dying on my seventh birthday

There had actually been a lot of uncertainty over whether or not I'd even make it to seven alive. The air raids had been fierce of late.

And a few weeks before my seventh birthday, I'd had a dream I was going to die a little boy—but it ended in excitement. The angel that had come to take my life away also happened to be super-duper sexy—which was the reason I'd never recounted the dream to my mum, knowing she'd ban me from dreaming naughty.

I did eventually draw the dream—and when the women of the house saw my drawing, instead of applauding, as they usually did, they asked me who the woman was. Why did she have a hook for a hand? Why was she standing in a graveyard? And why was she blonde?

When I told them it was the angel of death, they gasped and asked me to redraw her, only this time in black drapes, and faceless.

This in turn got me banned from staying up to watch the illegal satellite channels—which were my window on the world, my sanctuary. The channels showed uncensored Hollywood films, in black and white; the TV was installed by my mum's brother Salman but he never watched it.

Instead Adnan, Mum's other brother, was glued to the tube

whenever he got a break from service. We stayed up late, mesmerised by the white folks and their mysterious, alien activities.

'Marlon Marnrow. She is fantastic! Even in black and white she looks colourful,' he drooled.

I asked what would happen if we got caught watching foreign TV.

'Jail. Torture. Death. Who knows? One thing's for sure: a sordid end.'

'What's sordid, Uncle Adnan?'

'Bad, terrible, horrible,' he said. 'But don't think negative. Don't think about getting caught. Poker face, poker face, poker face. When I fight on the front line, I don't think to myself, *Oh, what happens if they catch me?* No. I think about survival. And, of course, about what sauce I'll put on my club sandwich if I ever make it back to base alive.'

He was a joker, but the sauce line made me hungry.

It turned out the vision of my death was just a mirage. Nanni made the birthday cake; I saved three months' pocket money to buy the candles, when really what I wanted to spend it on was blue jeans.

When I went to light the candles, Mum suggested, cheerfully, that I should wait till they dropped a bomb on us so they'd get lit up for free.

Blue jeans blues

The reason I wanted a pair of jeans so much was that I was sick of being mocked by the Iranian kids.

I wore a *dishdasha* and it made me the laughing stock of the town. My Farsi wasn't bad, and if only I had a pair of blue denims I was sure they'd stop calling me funny names. 'A is for Arab, B is for baboon,' they'd say. 'Shroud-wearing camel.' The names weren't actually that funny.

My cousins, who did wear jeans, fitted in so easily, fitted in with the ease of Vaseline. But Mum wanted me to be a proud Arab, and wear the *dishdasha* full-time. She also knew it would be impossible for me to save up for some jeans, so she made a deal with me: if I paid for them myself, I'd have her blessing to wear them. Clever lady.

I'd saved nearly enough twice, but each time I'd got close, I'd had to break the piggy bank because we needed food. The time I'd bought my birthday candles I'd splurged on a soccer ball too—another way to show the Persian boys that I was cool. That I could bring a ball, and we could *all* play.

I arrived with the soccer ball, the *dishdasha* tucked inside my pants, creating this unattractive, unruly bulge. 'How many months pregnant are you?' they asked. 'Did you eat Saddam Hussein?' Mansour, a ten-year-old whose father had been killed—martyred—last year, scoffed before he took my ball, withdrew a knife, and sliced my ball in two. He yelled at me to go back to my dirt hole.

Schools had been shutting down more and more regularly thanks to the heavy bombardments. By default, I didn't like school—no kid does, let alone a bullied one—but I was bored enough to crave it like an addict.

I spent the dusty days wandering the streets looking for the leather boots of fallen soldiers. When I found some, I'd take them back to the basement of our apartment, cut them carefully into the shapes of flags, paint them in flag colours, then jerry-rig them onto large sheets of newspaper and glue them on. When they had dried, I'd 'frame' them, not using glass, but plastic bags, and use the bootlaces to decorate the edges.

Then I'd use numberplates nicked from abandoned army jeeps to give each collage an 'ID'. I took the plates to the local blacksmith, who cut them up for free into individual letters and numbers—which I'd use to come up with a plausible name and death-date for the departed, and glue them to the canvas, something like A L I 9–9–1988.

After spending countless hours, I'd finished my twelfth piece. The number twelve is significant for a Muslim Shiite, since we believe there are twelve imams, descendants of the Prophet Muhammad, who continue his lineage. In the hope that this figure would bode well for my works, I finally took them to the local mosque, telling my mum I was going there to learn to read the Koran.

The mosque was small and beautiful, with aqua doors and entrance arch. It had a small fountain for ablution, a small hall for prayer. Its two minarets had been destroyed by bombs, which enhanced the appeal: people actually came here and prayed a bomb would drop right then, in which case they would die as martyrs. I didn't yet have those aspirations.

For the most part, though, it was a gathering place for men unfit for war and old people, which lent it a retirement village air. That makes it sound depressing—there was a real sense of community. People felt alive there, and they rarely discussed the war. They loved to reminisce about old times, just like old people everywhere—things like how good the football team was, pre-revolution.

I laid out my potato sack on the floor outside the doors, and set the Koran down next to me in case one of our neighbours, always nosy, happened to pass by.

The sun was not friendly. It was making me earn every cent. I'd sweated a solid river by the time my first potential mark arrived—a young man, who must've either been home on leave or had done a runner.

'Hey, kid,' he said. I hated being called a kid. What kid doesn't? While we were at it, hadn't this guy been a kid once? Didn't he remember how infuriating that word must've been? So why was he insulting me? The heat made me irritable. I decided to smile and respond in a way that might net me a sale.

'Good afternoon, sir! How are you today? How's things? Are you on leave? Perhaps you're an escapee?' I was rambling—a rush to be respectful.

'Where did you learn your manners?' he asked.

'Sorry, I didn't mean to *accuse* you of being an escapee, I just wanted to know if you *were* one. Obviously it's none of my business. Sorry.'

'You're selling this shit outside a mosque? Is this a place of business or a place of worship?'

It was one of those questions adults liked to ask that condemned you no matter how you responded. Maybe he really was an escapee, which would've pissed him off, knowing even a kid could see it. I was still thinking this over when, all in a flash, my artworks shattered under the young man's boots.

He stomped and stomped and stomped on them, and no matter how much I cried, he just didn't stop stomping on my work. They made a noise when breaking; I could hear they were in pain. The sounds made my heart clench like a fist.

A crowd had gathered, and I already knew they'd side with him, because he was a man, and I was just a kid. Because he looked like a pious soldier, and I looked like a rascal.

Because he was Persian and I was Arab—a little punk in a wet *dishdasha*. It was wet from the sweat; it was getting wetter from the tears, and I think I might have peed a little too.

And just then, an old mosque patron saw my pocket-sized Koran and stopped the mob from harassing me further. He picked me up and walked me back home, where I knew I'd get a belting. And that was the day I realised jeans were probably not for me. God wanted me to be an unfashionable outsider.

Six feet away from a killed soldier's face

On Saturdays, our family went to Golzare-Shohada, aka the Martyrs' Rose Garden. Saddam had burned most of the parks—along with the farm fields and oil rigs—but the Martyrs' Rose Garden was miraculously untouched. In my grandmother's view, God had sent His angels to protect the martyrs' *souls* because they'd failed to shield those martyrs' *bodies*.

'They work overtime, the angels,' she hummed after her nightly prayers. 'They've got a world full of ruin to save.'

Dozens of bodies came here on a daily basis. Young, old. Almost always men. Almost always with blood seeping through their shrouds.

That the park was a makeshift cemetery didn't bother us boys. We got to play tiggy and hide-and-seek all day.

'You're it!' I shouted as I elbowed my brother Moe Greene—to show him I was boss, I was older, I was stronger, and to get him back for eating my chocolate-spread sandwich, which he'd stolen when an air-raid siren provided a distraction. It had been in the fridge, clearly marked *Osamah's sandwich*.

Moe Greene didn't show pain. He wore the *dishdasha* like me, which teaches you to take various kinds of punishment. It also handicaps you in a game of tiggy; while our cousins Mehdi and Musty could run like gazelles in their jeans, we had to shuffle like penguins in the *dishdashas* and the added disadvantage of sandals.

We ran across patches of sand and dry, dead grass, weaving in between the palm trees that had somehow stayed alive through the searing summer temperatures of Abadan.

Despite being a literal loser, I was enjoying myself. The free air, the freedom to run about without watching for landmines—it was liberating. Just nearby, Mum, Nanni and my aunts joined a group of wailing women to read the Koran for the souls of the martyrs. They were all mothers, grandmothers and aunts of the deceased. And in one case, a mistress, who the other women shunned—the martyr's wife most pointedly and particularly. I didn't know the extent of the adultery, but even at seven, I'd heard the rumours circulating the cemetery that the mistress had got gifts from the front line and the wife had not. My uncle Adnan often brought me shell casings and disarmed grenades, so I imagined she'd got a necklace made from those same materials.

The mistress never showed her face, but I knew she was pretty from her soft voice and soft cries. The wife brayed like a donkey; the mistress cried melodically, almost as if she was composing her weeping on the go. For us kids, certain gravestones supplied the perfect cover; you could circle them endlessly and avoid becoming 'it'. But most of them were clogged up by the women.

Unattended gravestones were even better for playing hide-and-seek. Right now, for instance, I was hiding behind the oldest headstone in the park, which belonged to a fourteen-year-old soldier named Reza. His mother went there every Friday, performing her many rituals for brightening the spirit of her departed son.

She was always oblivious to our games of tiggy. Or so I thought. Maybe she didn't get mad because she could remember her own son, who not that long ago had played just like this, in this park, before it had become a shrine for boys like hers.

We had an unwritten rule not to hide behind children's graves. But desperate times called for desperate measures. I did a quick prayer to assuage the guilt, but the guilt remained. All I could do was stare into the picture of Reza's face, which had been engraved into the headstone.

He had a stunning smile. He must have brushed his teeth twice a day, for sure. I made a deal with myself that I would be more like Reza, brush twice a day, instead of my current twice-a-week habit—so lazy. If I died, I wanted kids hiding behind my tombstone to think, *Wow! Look at that smile.* An example for other youngsters. You could always look good, dead especially.

'Oi!' Moe Greene shouted, jolting me out of my fantasy. 'Move away from that tombstone.'

I laughed nervously. 'Okay, you found me.' My cousins caught up. They all looked at me with disappointment, and pity.

'What have we said about hiding behind baby graves?' yelled Moe Greene. 'You *idioto*!'

I stopped myself from crying. I was the oldest boy. But my throat was warm, trying to let out an explosion. I knew I couldn't hold it much longer.

'Osamah,' Nanni called, in the nick of time. 'Come over here.'

I wiped away the tears and trudged towards the women.

'*Oocha*, read this passage of the Koran. I don't know this one off by heart,' she said. She was illiterate, and could only read the passages she'd memorised. Lines had long ago hijacked her face. She had a tattoo on her upper lip. It was a symbol, and I didn't know what it meant. She lost her husband when my mum was seven.

I'd once asked Mum what it had been like to lose her dad at seven. I was seven, and my own dad was on the front line. 'You son of a shit,' she'd said. 'Why do you ask these questions? Two-legged goat, go sit and play.'

Nanni had called me over to read for a newly arrived body. It was shrouded, seeping blood, and on its way into the ground, being lowered by a group of men chanting 'God is Great' and 'Death to the Tyrant'. I had to invent some of the passage as I recited it, since I'd only been learning to read the Koran for the past year.

'Nanni, it's getting dark!' I said. 'I hate reading for a new body. It freaks me out.' The arrival of bodies in the park was so common that we always just carried on playing when they came. When I got close to a corpse, I felt sick in my stomach. I could smell the dead.

'Each verse you read from the Koran brightens their soul,' she replied.

The idea of brightening the soul fascinated me, even though I couldn't explain it to my brain.

I went to go on reading, but before I could, one of the men lost his grip on the shroud and slipped into the open grave. He pulled the corpse in after him and it landed right on his face. 'Fucking vagina!' he screamed.

The religious chants stopped instantly. Nanni covered my ears. But I'd already heard it.

The other men tried to pretend their friend had shouted something holy, but in the open grave, with the corpse on him, he was still freaking out, still yelling like a schoolboy.

'Get this vagina corpse off me!' he cried. My ears were poorly muffled. He shoved the body off him, violently. And just like that, the shroud opened.

I threw up. Not on the corpse, thank God, but on Nanni's lap. The martyr's head was so flat it looked like an open book. A red book, a messy book that looked nothing like a face. The mouth was wide open. It had no eyes.

'Nanni,' I said quietly. 'When we read the Koran, does it just brighten his soul, or does it heal his face too?'

No answer. I wondered if I'd be in trouble for vomiting on her lap. If reading the Koran was in fact meant to heal the martyr's face, I wouldn't want to be the one doing it. It'd take two years just to bring the martyr's eyes back.

THE DAY GOD DIED

Mashhad, Iran, 2013

There are more felafel stands in Mashhad than there are restaurants in Sydney. So it's not strange that my dad and I have ended up at one where a man happens, in some small but crucial way, to need our help. The man is lucky because my father likes to help a stranger out.

This is an unusual way of living in the world, as the next week of my life is about to demonstrate.

The man is in his fifties, mostly bald; what hair he has is white. He's talking to his three children, two girls and a boy; one of the daughters is swinging from his arms. They are pleading with him to buy them 'regular' felafels—not halves, not one piece of bread with just sauce and no salads. Soft drink, too. They're thirsty. They play the promise card: he promised them today he'd buy regular felafel and drink.

The man tries to shush the children, likely from embarrassment. He tries to whisper that he *can't* buy these things, but he can't even whisper—have you ever tried to speak with subtlety to three hungry kids? They keep hassling him, chasing the meal. The man is distraught, even anguished.

No one pays him any mind. Mashhad is full of people who look just like this.

My father and I haven't been eating street food often since coming to Iran three weeks ago, but every now and then we forgo the fine dining for the grubby treat—it just tastes a little better knowing it isn't that good for you.

I'm fidgeting, uneasy. I know what Dad's craving: a double felafel, pickles, tomato, no sauce. I want the same, plus mustard. And we both want the obligatory Coke, straight out of the bottle. How can we possibly order this much food? Not here, in front of the man. Not in front of his kids.

So I make a choice. I reach for my wallet, feeling heroic, flashing it to Dad, to make sure he sees the generous gift I'm about to bestow. After all, in Australian dollars, a felafel with Coke is around forty cents. But just as I'm about to pull out a wad of cash, Dad grabs my forearm and slides the wallet back.

He tells me, in Arabic, so the man can't understand: 'Son, is the man begging? No. He is a working man, and a handout would be a slap in his face; it would rid him of his dignity. And his children will never forget that they saw a stranger give their father cash.'

I understand. 'Right. Sorry, Dad.'

'Just keep talking to me.'

So I keep murmuring in Arabic, pointless small talk, while Dad quietly slips a 50,000-toman note out of his own pocket. This is the equivalent of eighteen Australian bucks.

He ever so gently lets the note glide out of his hand. 'Keep talking,' he says. We do, and then, a moment later, Dad taps the old man on the shoulder.

'Excuse me, sir,' he says, in Farsi. 'I believe you dropped some money.'

The man looks at the floor. It's a huge denomination.

'Sorry, that's not mine,' he says.

Dad looks him closely in the eyes.

'No, sir,' he says firmly. 'I saw. It fell from your pocket, when you were swinging your daughter…'

The broken man regards my father. He conjures a smile.

◆ ◆ ◆

On the minibus as we're heading back to the hotel, Dad takes my arm and places it behind his back so it acts as a cushion. It's been a long morning, and my father needs a nap.

As he's dozing off, he starts to mumble nonsense about how much he misses Mum. How, in thirty years of marriage, he's never told her he loves her.

'But I know she knows I love her,' he says. 'She has known since day one. It's the actions, in any case. But it would've been nice to tell her…'

And then off he goes, head against the window, the streets of Mashhad whipping past him as he finally rests.

◆ ◆ ◆

Dad falls into bed. 'Osamah, *habibi*, I'm exhausted. Will you go have dinner on your own?'

'Sure, Dad.'

He smiles. I close the curtains, turn the heating up and head to the hotel restaurant alone.

It's the first time in weeks I'm eating without Dad. It's an alien feeling. There's a pretty girl at an opposite table; we trade brief smiles. I rush through my food, check a few emails on the lobby wi-fi. I tell my cousin in England I'll be seeing her soon, on the next leg of our trip; she's as excited as I am. I haven't seen her—or her five sisters—in twenty years.

We've gone a solid couple of days with little sleep, and I realise I'm tired too. So I head back upstairs, to study a little and maybe have a nap.

I swipe my card, leave the lights off so as not to wake Dad. I walk in quietly. Something is not right. I look at the bed where Dad is sleeping and I see that he's not there. Or—

I look at the bed again. A rush of goosebumps hits me. My body is talking to me, but I don't know what the signals mean. Dad lies flat on the bed, but still, he isn't there. I whisper, 'Oh, fuck,' so quietly I can barely hear myself speak. I launch myself at the body and try to wake him up. I shake him hard, kissing his neck.

'Dad! Wake up! Dad! Please! Dad! Wake up!' I get angry and loud. 'I'm sorry if I'm yelling at you but you're not listening to me! Wake up!'

It's true: he's not listening. I cradle his head in my arms. Suddenly, I sense a presence behind me and turn around. There are a dozen strangers. When did they get here? I can't quite make out their words—but they're all giving instructions, about what to do, how to keep his airways clear, how to resuscitate. I won't let his head go. I keep hugging him, kissing him.

I must've been yelling so loud the whole floor of the hotel is here.

I look at my watch. I want to know exactly what time it is.

I picture every single friend and family member and think: *What are you doing right this very moment?*

I feel a hand on my shoulder. The pretty girl from the restaurant. I think, why is she touching me? This is Iran. It's illegal here. I beg the girl to tell me that this is all a dream. She just looks at me, crying. She is crying more than me.

The paramedics arrive and forcefully remove me from my dad.

They run all sorts of procedures. One of them turns to me and says words I don't understand. 'What does passed away mean?' I ask. Surely not the same thing as it means in English. The man's making no sense, even in Farsi.

'He's been gone an hour.'

I beseech them to wake him. It's *their job* to wake him up. But they place him on a trolley bed and drape him in a sheet.

❖ ❖ ❖

I notice that the ambulance is a Mercedes. I feel the dashboard. My brother has one of these. Bigger than this one. He moves furniture in it; I've helped him many times. I wonder what it would be like to drive a van with a dead body in it. I start mumbling something about how I drive a van just like this back in Australia. How Dad actually bought it for my brother Mohammed, aka Moe Greene, to help him get back on his feet after a rough divorce.

The driver doesn't say anything. He just drives, with the siren on. Does this mean surgeons might save him? Surely something can reverse this, some expensive German device.

The traffic moves slowly. Don't people know what an ambulance siren means? I ask the driver what the time is. He checks his watch. I check mine.

I wait in reception at the hospital. I stand, sit, stand again. I pace up and down. Remember, this is all just a dream.

It's now close to midnight. About 6 am back home. I have to call my family and tell them, but I can't. *Hey, guys, how's it going? By the way, Dad's gone.* I am sure the doctors will come bearing good news. They will say the paramedics were ill-equipped to do proper tests.

I pace up to a group of nurses congregating behind the counter. I ask one what the time is. 'Are you always this anxious?' she says.

'No, I'm not used to seeing my father die, you see,' I tell her, anxious, not believing my own words.

'I know, you are the Australian, yes?'

'Yes.'

'His body is being examined.'

'He will be alive in minutes, yes?'

The nurse looks at me closely. 'Have you got some wires loose?'

'No,' I protest. 'You think I'm crazy, but I'm just thinking of modern medicine. You see, in Australia, science is a big thing. It can heal people and it can save people. You can explain life with it.' I fidget. 'Do you have the time?'

She is silent for a minute. 'Get this boy a glass of water,' she says.

A doctor approaches. He looks a lot older than Dad.

'Are you the relative of the Australian man?'

'Yes.'

'What are you to him?'

'I don't know,' I say. 'His eldest son. But he was my father, he was everything. He was God, I think.'

'Be careful who you say that to,' the doctor says. 'Don't go saying that to the police when they interview you, for one thing. I trained in Europe, I know you don't mean apostasy, but they can hang you for that.' He hands me a sheet of paper. 'I've estimated the time of death.'

'No.'

'No? No to what?'

'No to everything.'

'Son. We all die. It's our destiny. I just need you to sign this.'

I look down at the death notice. Am I really doing this? This morning, we were drinking Coke at a felafel stand.

'Sorry, doctor,' I say. 'Can you sign it for me?'

'What kind of son are you? Sign it!' he snaps. 'Your father deserves this, at the very least. Now sign it, damn it!'

I look at the paper and something inside me wakes up. The doctor's words echo. *I must take care of him after his death.* When the doctor hands me a pen, I take it and sign the sheet.

❖ ❖ ❖

Time has stopped, but my watch keeps ticking. I'm still in reception at the hospital. I finally call my younger brother, Ali.

'Hey. How's Iran going?' he asks me. 'It's Sunday morning here.'

'Yeah, I'm good. Iran's good. It's Saturday night here. Hey, sorry if I'm disturbing you.'

'No, I'm on the way to work.' Ali works early on Sundays. 'Running late, actually.'

'That's no good, running late is never good, I'm always running late,' I say. 'Hey, listen, if you're driving, just pull over for a second.'

A long pause.

'Go on,' he says.

'Okay, so I think Dad's not in a good situation. He had a heart attack and died.'

'What do you mean?'

'I think he's not alive anymore.'

'No, man.' He softly exhales.

His *no* echoes like a soundtrack from a horror movie.

'It's pretty much a hundred per cent. Sorry, bro, I think it's real,' I whisper.

'No, man! What about the doctors? People have heart attacks all the time. He's only fifty.'

'I have a police interview, then I have to see what the procedure is to bring him home. None of this "bury him in Iraq" and "Iraq is holy ground" bullshit. Okay?'

'Yeah, yeah.' I don't know if he gets it. 'Sure, bro. Are you in Qom?'

'Mashhad.'

'But it's freezing there now, no? It's crowded. Are you going to get things done?'

'Yes to your last question. I think it's cold to your first. Listen, I have to bring him back in the next few days, my visa's gonna expire. Shit, can you hear me talk about Dad like this? Ali, do not tell anyone. Do not tell a soul. Don't tell Mum. Not yet. Let me finish the procedures here. There could be a few hurdles.'

I hang up and sit down. I watch the wall clock ticking.

Two hours later, it's still ticking. I've never noticed the white fluorescent lights at a hospital like this before. They are super bright. An officer in military uniform greets me. He invites me to an interview room in another part of the hospital. He's eating a submarine sandwich. He says a detective is on his way.

He squeezes out his condolences. He assures me it's just procedure. Since Dad is a foreigner, they want it done by the book.

They've also learned that Dad is the head cleric in Melbourne, and a representative of the major scholars of Iran. So they're taking extra caution, to avoid the local media out of respect. He ushers me into the interview room and tells me to sit down.

'Wherever you're comfortable,' he says.

I look around. There's a table and a large chair, probably for the officer, and two smaller wooden chairs. They're identical. I do eeny, meeny, miny, moe and pick one. I can't believe my brain is doing this.

The officer bites through his sandwich, salad hanging out of his mouth. He's overweight. Through his thick lenses, I can't quite see his eyes.

He lectures me about burying Dad next to Imam Reza. 'Mashhad is a holy ground. It is of great fortune for your father to have died not only on this sacred land, but during the memorial of the great imam's death as well.'

'Thank you for the offer,' I say, 'but I have to inform you I'll be taking Dad to be buried back where his family lives.'

The officer chews through his submarine like a wild mule. He talks with his mouth full. 'Listen carefully, son. There's a few things you'll have to do to get your father out of here.' I brace for a litany of tasks. 'There's a lot of things to do,' he repeats, vaguely. 'I wouldn't have a clue. We don't have many of these cases.'

'How long do you think the procedure will take?' I ask him. 'My visa expires next Saturday.'

'What are we now, Saturday? It'll be touch and go. You'll have to get it extended.'

'I already have,' I say. 'I'm not allowed another one.'

'Yeah, sorry,' he says. 'Just try and get everything done as fast as you can. Okay, I want you to write. Can you write?'

'Yes.'

'In Farsi?'

'Yes, sir.' I knew that was what he meant.

'Good boy,' he says. 'Write down all the events. Right up until your discovery of the deceased. What you did this morning, all that. We can use this as your statement, so be detailed.'

So I start. I haven't written anything formal in Persian in a long time, but the events are so fresh in my mind that they come without a hurdle. The officer keeps chewing and keeps talking as I write.

'Don't worry about your father's death. We'll all die,' he says. 'Life is a shithole anyway. It's sewage. Believe me, I wish I was dead. How old was your father?'

I'm trying to focus. 'Fifty, I think.'

'Wow! Eight years younger than me. I'm going to die one day, too. This life just isn't worth it. I swear, I envy your father. Take this afternoon, for instance. I'm lining up to get a burger. I tell the clerk I want mayonnaise, and what sauce does he put? Aioli! I'm telling you, life's shit. Worthless. Can you believe it? No mayonnaise. It's wonderful, your father doesn't have to see all this suffering anymore.'

I sit, completely stunned. I want to stand up and choke him. On the other hand, I pity him. I want him to see a therapist—and I want to pay for it too.

But the other thing is, what he said was stupid, but it was quite funny too. I want to laugh. But I don't.

❖ ❖ ❖

Two hours later, the detective arrives. Aioli Cop lets him in.

He's a young man, bearded, with a strong regional accent. He goes through the condolences in such a way that it's clear it's just routine.

He asks me to recount the story—how I found Dad, what happened earlier. I tell him I've already written the story and given it to his colleague.

He shrugs. 'That wasn't necessary. I have to write it down.'

For fifty minutes, I go over it again. I sign a paper, stating that he's ruled me out as a suspect. I ask how long the procedure will take.

'I hear you want to take the body back to Australia,' he says. 'Why not bury him here? Religious place. Next to the imam.'

'We have no family here.'

'So? He died here. It has a meaning. Put him in holy grounds.'

I wonder if he's saying this to give himself an easier job, or if the sentiment is genuine. I don't know.

The detective tells me he doesn't know either—what exactly the procedures are. He suggests I play it by ear from department to department. He assures me the job will take no more than a couple of days. I breathe a little easier; the last thing I want is to serve a prison sentence while Dad lies in an Iranian morgue. The detective stamps the paper. He seals it in an envelope. He hands it to me. He tells me to take it to Kalantari 27, a police division. Aioli Cop looks surprised. A police car should take me, he says. Or the detective should take the form there himself. It's his job.

The detective contests this. It's past midnight, and the police cars are all out of action at this time. He asks if I'll have a problem finding my own way to the Kalantari 27. He tries to ease the burden: it's only a half-hour drive.

I'm so bewildered I can't reply. It's late at night, or actually early the next day, in a city of millions. I couldn't even find my own hotel.

'You're a big boy,' he says. 'Your Farsi is better than mine.'

I finally speak up. 'Sir, it's not just getting the address and a taxi. I don't even know the name of this hospital. And what if nobody's there to take the envelope? How do I contact you? I haven't been in Iran for close to thirteen years.'

'Thirteen years. Is that how long you've been in Australia?'

'No, we left in 1995.'

The detective gets excited. 'Wow. What is Australia like?'

'Excuse me?'

'Is it like they say?'

'I don't know. Yeah, it's good. But, the envelope—'

'Are there a lot of kangaroos and girls in bikinis?' he says, wide-eyed.

'Sort of. Sir—'

'Oh, yes. So, get a taxi.' He writes down the address. 'And tell him you want Kalantari 27. He will know.'

'Sir, I can't.' My hands are shaking. 'I can't even hold this envelope.'

'You are being a difficult young man,' says the detective. 'Maybe it's all the privileges in Australia? Anyway, as they say, don't give the tailor's work to the baker. He'll burn the clothes and say, "Look, I coloured it for you."'

He gets on his two-way radio and tries to get us a ride. No luck. He was dropped off by a patrol car, and this is the end of his shift. He hints that I should probably chip in for his taxi—after all, if it wasn't for me, he'd be walking home from his own division.

I just collapse, put my head in my hands. I don't know what's happening here. I have a police officer worried about aioli sauce and a detective concerned about cab fare.

◆ ◆ ◆

An hour later, the police radio crackles. There are no vehicles available. The detective needs to take the 'suspect' to Kalantari 27 in a cab.

He holds his breath for a long second. He blurts into the radio: 'I am out of my depth here.' He doesn't do death cases—worse, a foreign national. 'I'm in burglary. This is too much. I don't even know what questions to ask him. The kid's a mess. So am I.'

I can't make out what they tell him. He switches off the radio and gestures for me to follow.

The taxi navigates us through the dark night. 'They will tell you everything in Kalantari,' he says. 'But look, see how easy it all would've been if you had just got that cab.'

He tells the driver to hang tight until we finish our business at the cop shop. Inside Kalantari 27, the detective flashes his badge. We take the stairs to the third floor, where the detective briefs a sergeant. The sergeant appraises me with an air of displeasure.

'Why not bury him here?' he says.

I grit my teeth. 'I want to take him home.'

'You call *Australia* home?'

I can't help it: my brain calls up the song 'I Still Call Australia Home'. I feel like breaking into it, shouting out the words. It feels so ridiculous, I want to laugh again.

The sergeant says only the chief can authorise the release of the body, and even then it's only the release from the coroner's to the morgue. In my mind, an avalanche falls, heavy and suffocating.

'Come back in the morning,' the sergeant says. 'The chief comes in at six o'clock.'

The detective hops in my taxi, catching a ride home.

'I thought you lived in walking distance,' I enquire.

'From my own division,' he says. 'This is homicide.'

The detective and the taxi driver talk about politics. They get into a heated debate about the sanctions on Iran. The driver can't get spare parts for the taxi anymore; they're from Germany. Every driver he knows has been hit hard. Black-market parts cost too much. Fuel prices have risen threefold to compensate for the lack of exports.

The detective takes the government's side, but shares the driver's pain. He had three children in private school; he had to take them out. Just getting food on the table is luxury enough. I zone out and look outside. I can't see much of the darkened town. The stars are blocked by clouds. It's freezing, not that I feel much of it. I look at the time.

The detective gets out near a block of old apartments. He tells the driver I'll take care of the fare. He looks at me to confirm. I'm over it, too tired. I nod, and thank him for all his overtime.

The driver pulls out. He tries to talk about Australia. I want to humour him, but I don't have the energy. He doesn't know what's happened. He pulls out his phone and tries to show me a video clip of a monkey taking a peeled banana then squirting its contents back in the person's face. I'm not really in the mood for this, but I try to be polite.

At the hotel, the driver goes on his *taarof* rant—in Persian culture, it's customary to decline any offer up to three times before accepting it—'No, I don't want the money! You're a guest.' I can't be bothered with this either, so I pay him too much and leave.

The concierge offers me a fresh room. I accept it. But first of all, I have to take care of Dad's things. I see his turban—still ready to wear from our outing yesterday morning. I don't want it to crumble and lose its shape, so I place it carefully on top of everything else in my backpack and avoid zipping the top.

I call my wife from my new room. I tell her Dad's died, over and over again, insisting that it's true. I try to calm her, but I really can't. She's crying; I am too. But my mind is busy about the task ahead, so I contain my tears. I hate myself for doing this. I've become a Westerner. If anyone from the Middle East saw my gentle tears, they'd think I was happy my father was dead.

We talk until my credit runs out. I stare at the dead phone. I shower in the foetal position and stay there a long time.

A MERCILESS MAGIC

Abadan City, Iran, 1988

Drunk Russian

It was the height of winter and Moe Greene and I were slowly going out of our minds, waiting for the next air-raid siren to sound. My tough-as-nails Uncle Adnan—that lover of illegal television—devised a game to keep us occupied. He called the game Drunk Russian because one needed to be drunk to enjoy it. We were sober.

One needed to be drunk because participants were required to stand in the snow, barefoot, stripping one layer each minute. We were allowed to begin with a maximum of ten layers of clothing, so by the time we were down to underwear, we'd endured a good ten minutes in temperatures of six below zero. My toddler brother, who was too young for such tortures, watched from the apartment, clapping and cheering.

I did not know what the word 'drunk' meant, but I did know drink was prohibited and punishment ranged from lashings to imprisonment. The promise of punishment made the game all the more appealing. What was this magical potion, and what might cause Iran to ban it? Why did adults only discuss it in a hushed, delicious manner?

I had more pressing problems. I was down to my singlet.

Moe Greene was down to his underwear, and declared himself the winner. He started jumping up and down while doing a shimmy.

'I'm the winner, I'm a sinner! You're a snoozer, you're a loser!'

Whenever Moe said he was a sinner, I got nervous—it meant he was about to do something naughty. And there it was: he took off his underwear, revealing his bare butt.

He started shaking himself back and forth in a victorious slashing motion, a very unpious manoeuvre that swung his genitals like a pendulum.

'Check out my cherries dangling!' he yelled. 'Have you seen cherries grow in snow? In your face, jerkface! I'm the Russian drunk! Woot woot!'

Mum would have to chase after him with a broom. It was procedure. He didn't care. He loved the attention—especially from all our girl cousins, who watched his antics, looked away, then watched some more, in increasing horror.

We loved Drunk Russian simply because we wanted to replicate Uncle Adnan's valour and temerity, which were legendary in his ancient home city of Bakhtaran. He'd shot himself in the foot—literally—to get leave as a wounded soldier so he could reunite with the village girl he'd fallen in love with. He lost his toe, but felt the wound was a minor trade-off.

He had many stories. But my favourite one was this:

It was operation night, and Adnan was squeezed inside the hole he'd dug into the side of a hill. His eyes fixed on a star that had been winking at him all evening through the cloudless sky. He winked back at it, wondering if the hole was about to be his grave—this tiny space, a world away from the world he understood.

He was in the Tank-Diffusion Unit, the TDU, a commando corps of nut jobs who got off on the thought of suicide.

Their mission was simple: curtail trample damage from Iraqi tank fire before they penetrated Iran's front line. When the hordes of Iraqi tanks had overcome the landmines, that was when the TDU clocked on for work.

They planted live bombs, by hand, under moving enemy tanks—which they secured in one slippery socket underneath the tank. Lose concentration for a hair's-breadth of a second and you were simply dead: the bomb would go off too late, alerting your enemies to your presence. They worked in groups of five or six, so that if one commando screwed up, only a small number of men would go down with him. If someone fumbled, his best bet was to grab on to the tank and let it drag him so the explosion would go off as far away as possible, and not give away the positions of the rabbit holes.

Now, Adnan heard the enemy tanks beginning to rumble through the desert. The winking star winked out for good, vanishing in the dust cloud stirred up by the approaching tanks, but Adnan thought the star was frightened, that it had no wish to witness what was about to come.

He closed his eyes, trying to focus. But all that he could picture was the face of the Iranian girl he'd met in the village a few weeks ago. His Iraqi origins made him a priceless asset to the Iranians; he could speak the language, knew how the Iraqis designed their attacks and, more importantly, he knew how they thought, how their brains worked. But even though he'd fought endlessly for the Iranians, he would always be seen as an Iraqi. How would he convince her father to let her marry him, an Arab?

A MERCILESS MAGIC

The earth began to vibrate—a tank was barrelling up the hill. He pushed the girl from his mind, and spoke his oath out loud: 'Martyrdom first, all else last. Martyrdom first, all else last.'

In seconds, the tank was on him. He reached up with the mine, trying to find the socket. His hands shook. His fingers were cold. The mine wouldn't go in.

It would self-activate in seconds. He had little choice. He lifted his body and grabbed the rails for one final joyride. He spoke his last prayers silently. Out loud, he just said, 'Shit.'

His teeth chattered as the tank dragged him. He clutched the bomb in one hand. The tank neared the top of the hill. Still, the bomb didn't explode. Once the tank passed the hill, it would hurtle down at a thousand miles an hour. There was no way he could keep hanging on at that speed.

Still gripping the rail with one hand, he shoved the bomb under his helmet and hauled himself to the ladder that ran down the side of the tank. He dragged himself up the rungs and sat astride the vehicle, took three deep breaths and grabbed a grenade from his utility bag. He lifted the latch, yanked it open.

He jumped inside the tank.

It was dark inside, but he'd been in the dark night a long time. It smelled of metal, sweat and gunpowder. Four soldiers, all caught off guard.

He waved the grenade at the soldiers and started shouting in Arabic. 'I have a grenade and we're all going to hell!'

One of the Iraqis put his hands over his head, dropping a flask of alcohol, which spilled across the floor. The driver was too shocked to stop. The third soldier pointed his rifle directly at Uncle Adnan. Uncle Adnan prepared himself to pull the pin on the grenade. He caught the eyes of the fourth soldier—the commander, he could tell.

'Halt!' yelled the commander.

Adnan was not about to move.

The men turned to the commander, not knowing what to do. Slowly now, the third soldier lowered his rifle. The drunk soldier dropped his arm. The driver stopped the tank, and the commander stepped forward. He threw his arms around Adnan, in a suffocating bear hug. Adnan started laughing with the excitement of a man who has stared at certain death and won the staring contest. He was embracing one of Iraq's most wanted generals, Colonel Majid Ghaith, who also happened to be his former high-school biology teacher.

'It's been ten years,' said the colonel.

'You're looking fantastic, Mr Ghaith! What a surprise.'

'It's Colonel Ghaith now, actually, but—thank you—I don't look good at all. I've lost weight, and lung cancer might kill me before the war does.'

Adnan shrugged. 'Losing weight is actually a massive thing in America. I have seen it on our dish. Every day a new diet.'

'Fucking Americans,' said the colonel. 'Started this whole mess.'

They caught up on Mrs Ghaith. She was doing well; the colonel dreamed about her delicious lamb kebab on a bed of rice every night. Adnan dreamed of finding a proper toilet and taking a proper shit. 'Excuse my language, sir, but the lack of plumbing in the desert is worse than the bombs.'

'That's exactly why I eat once a day only,' the colonel said. 'Taking your pants off behind a sack of rice is never pleasant.'

The other soldiers were completely stunned. One of them picked up the flask; they all took massive swigs, which can be the only way to process a scenario like this.

But then the colonel's face turned. He squinted at Adnan, studying him. There was only so much luck in the world. Adnan paled.

The colonel took a step towards him, moustache nearly touching his nose. 'Tell me,' he said icily. 'Who would you support in the World Cup qualifiers? Iraq or Iran?'

Adnan didn't hesitate. 'Iraq, of course.'

The colonel continued studying him. Then slapped him lightly on the face. 'That's my boy. I'm glad to hear you haven't completely defected.'

Adnan rolled his eyes. 'Of course not! Our soccer team comes before our mothers. We didn't make the '86 Mexico finals but, God willing, Italy 1990, if this war stops.'

'God willing, my son. God willing.'

Before Adnan left the tank, he told the colonel his situation—back home in the village, the lovely Iranian girl.

'Don't marry her!' said the colonel. 'Not if she's a good cook. I've missed my wife's cooking for forty-seven months now. I've missed her, but not as much as that lamb kebab on rice.'

Colonel Majid Ghaith then ordered his navigating officer to drive the tank miles away—giving Uncle Adnan the best chance he could to get back to his unit. The pair embraced one last time, wishing each other well.

Later that chilly winter, the Iranian army celebrated the capture and execution of Colonel Majid Ghaith.

Rooftop views of air raids

I was down to my singlet in a game of Drunk Russian with Moe Greene when the scream of the air-raid siren shot through the streets of Abadan.

My toddler brother was standing at our bedroom window, clapping as he watched us play.

I looked at Moe Greene, who was down to his underpants. 'Should we go to the rooftop?' I said.

We did this constantly, whenever we heard the sirens—despite our mother's just as constant, very insistent rebuke. The fighter planes were mythic birds, hypnotic, powerful, beautiful. I loved to stand on the roof and watch buildings go up in flames; the aquamarine sky frolicked pink. It was a merciless magic. It was free, front-row tickets to fireworks that burned all night.

We made our way up there.

Mum was onto us. 'Osamah! Mohammad! Get down before I come and kill you myself!' she screamed. I loved her abuses; I loved the insults she yelled. She was the most loving person in my entire world. I wondered what would happen if a bomb was dropped on me. Would I see my guts gush out my body? Would I be cool to look at then? Would the girl across the street find my charred remains and say, 'That's the Arab boy who never said hi to me'?

'Keep going,' whispered Moe. 'Mum will hit us. But she won't, you know, *kill*-kill us.'

But her voice was getting closer and I convinced him to listen. We ran downstairs to join our mother and our aunties, who were shepherding dozens of people into the bunkers.

We huddled in. Moe was gloating about winning Drunk Russian, but people weren't paying enough attention. To correct this, he started slowly pulling down his undies to reveal his bum crack. I remember the disgusted looks on the girls all around.

Then a series of bombs rocked the bunker for the longest time. All banter and laughter and chatter stopped. Debris fell through the air holes. The girls and boys cried; the women too. Our home was finally nothing but a smouldering carcass.

And then it hit me, the worst thing, the irreparable thing. My youngest brother was still up there, transfixed by the noisy, colourful sky. Mum's headcount had come two minutes too late.

Mum never spoke about that day ever again, though her moist eyes painted melancholic pictures of lament at random.

A cow on the last day of the war

Dad was still not home, but the promise was he would be home soon. On this last day of the war, the oil rigs were burning, making a hot day hotter. They would burn for a long time.

And there was a cow—one cow, indifferently grazing.

And then a long train of Iraqi POWs, all with their hands on their heads, walking in single file.

All life had drained from their bodies, these weary hordes. The Iranian company leading them looked equally worn. The only difference was the Iraqis all had bushy moustaches; the Iranians had beards. Beards versus moustaches. That's all.

The Iranians pointed their guns at the Iraqis and told them to keep walking, in way-past-reluctant tones.

Where they had come from, where they were going—all of this a mystery.

I just saw soldiers leading soldiers while the cow chewed on the shrubs.

THE TALL MALE WAS OF EXCELLENT HYGIENE

Mashhad, Iran, 2013: six days until visa expires

When I finally drag myself out of the shower, it's 5 am. I get dressed and go downstairs.

The concierge kindly reminds me that I am to check out this morning (and since the hotel's booked to the rafters, I really do have to). Dad and I were meant to head back to Qom today. I have a plane to catch. What with the Imam Reza commemoration and all, how will I get another flight? I have to take the police chief the envelope. I assure the receptionist I'll be back.

I cab it to Kalantari 27, where activity has quadrupled since last night. The guards at the door frisk me. I head up to see the chief.

The chief is out on patrol. Instead, I get a sergeant. I explain my situation—the hotel, the flight, the body. He dunks a sugar cube in his tea and shuts his eyelids for two whole seconds. He reopens them, nodding his head slightly. He takes a sip of his tea and goes on with his business.

At eight-thirty the chief shows up and heads to his office. He closes the door before I can get a word in. He's a short man—that's all I have time to absorb.

Just after ten o'clock, the chief opens his door. He twitches his index finger to call me into the room.

'So you had nothing to do with the man's death?' He asks.

'The man,' I say. 'My dad.'

'Hmm,' he says. 'Son, do you know how many family homicide cases I've done?' He says this so dramatically I have to stifle a laugh. He squints his eyes and studies me. I'm too worn out to protest. I just have to wait until he's done X-raying my mind.

He asks me to go through the events again. I walk him through them. As I speak, he cross-checks my story against the statement taken yesterday by the burglary detective who was so 'out of his depth'.

'So you didn't hit your father?' the chief says.

I'm stunned. 'What?'

'Says here you were hitting your father.'

'Oh, no, no,' I say. 'That was a reaction. I wanted to wake him up, you see.'

'Have you had physical altercations with your father before?'

'No!' I say. 'I hit him because he was dead and I didn't want him to be dead.'

He opens his drawer, takes out a stamp and stamps the statement. He scribbles a note on the paper.

'Take this to the coroner's,' he says. 'This is not your release yet. Since you're a foreigner and your father was an important man abroad, I'm taking extra caution. I need an official cause of death. If the cause of death is consistent with your statement, I will sign the release to the morgue so they can give you a burial permit. Then you can take it from there.'

I thank him and rush out. I hail a cab outside the Kalantari. It stops for me. Good news: I just have to shout 'coroner' and the driver flings open the door.

There's a long line at the coroner's. I line up behind everyone else. Forty minutes later, a man behind the counter takes the paper the chief gave me and goes out to search for my file. He comes back with the death certificate and tells me to take it back to the Kalantari.

I run out and find a taxi. It's way past my checkout time. I call information, get the hotel's number and talk to the receptionist. He tells me the people who have booked the room are on their way.

Could he take my belongings out? I ask him.

He consults with a supervisor, then confirms: this, they can do.

I hang up and read the cause of death. Cardiac arrest. The last paragraph catches my eye: 'The tall male was of excellent hygiene.' Why would they include that? It's tattooed on my mind.

Back at the Kalantari, it only takes the chief another thirty-eight minutes to open his office door. He stamps the paper and wishes me well. 'I could tell you are not the kind who would kill his father, but my instinct has been off since my divorce.' He hopes there are no hard feelings.

Back to the coroner's again.

Official closing time is 4 pm. It's after three by now. My flight's at seven-fifty. I can't focus on that right now.

At the coroner's, the guard tells me to come back in the morning. I explain my situation as rapidly as I can. He goes inside and talks to the man who found the death certificate. The man recognises me, and nods his head. I sit down in the hall. A lot of people are waiting. I hear causes of death called. Every one is drug-related, no matter how old people are.

Finally, I hear my name. I head to the counter.

'Where are the court papers?' the man says, clapping once and showing me his palms.

'What court papers?' I ask.

'These are the police papers. Isn't your father a foreign national?'

'Yes, but no one told me—'

'Didn't I tell you to take the death certificate to the courts? I think I told you.'

'No, sir, you did not.'

'Well. You have to take the chief's paper and get it released through the court.'

'I have a visa expiring on Saturday.'

'Don't get rowdy, just do as I say.'

'They'll be shut today.'

'So do it tomorrow. Don't complicate things.'

'I have to fly back to Qom tonight, I haven't got a place to stay—'

'You think you're the only one with problems?'

I can't think. I just take the chief's stamped statement and take a taxi back to the hotel. More than a day has passed and I still haven't told Mum. I want to be sure what's happening first, but the pressure's mounting.

The hotel manager apologises for being unable to accommodate me tonight; the religious festival means the whole city's booked out. I take Dad's suitcase and walking stick, and head out in search of a room for the night.

It's just after 7 pm and my body's shutting down. I've barely slept in days, and haven't had anything to eat in all this time; nothing to drink either, except the glass of water at the hospital last night. I stop at a felafel stand and grab two sandwiches. I remember the last felafel stand—not so long ago, Dad was giving a man who was down on his luck some money. I wonder where he is right now. What he and his children are doing. I check the time and swallow the sandwiches. I don't even feel them go down, so I order another two. I down those with little chewing.

Five sandwiches later, I go hotel hunting again. I try more than thirty hotels, motels, hotels, serviced apartments—nothing. I look at my watch again. It's midnight already.

Snow falls, stiffening the tips of my fingers. I must've walked over twenty kilometres, wearing a backpack, dragging luggage. I have to take a gamble. I cab it back to our old hotel.

I casually enter the lobby and collapse on the couch. It's *incredibly* comfortable. I sink right in, feeling the enervation drain out. The staff here know me; they know I have no reservation for the night. I look nervously at the receptionist. He catches my glance for half a second. He gives me a slight nod, gets back to his business, and lets me close my eyes.

CHEEKY SON OF A CLERIC MAN

Qom, Iran, 1995

For Shiites, Qom was one of the holiest cities in Iran. It was home to the prestigious *hawza 'ilmiyya*, the largest Shiite seminary in the world, and the shrine to Hazrat Ma'sooma—the eighth imam's sister, and also the granddaughter of the Prophet.

In other words, it was turban festival. It's also where my family moved after the eight-year war. You don't have to be a geography enthusiast to see how bizarre this would be to a seven-year-old kid. During the war, we lived in Abadan, on the Iraqi border, always feeling the mortar shells caress our ears. And now, here we were, in central Iran, about 200 kilometres from Tehran—probably the safest place we could've been during the war, which now happened to be over.

But I wasn't a seven-year-old kid anymore. I was officially a teen. I'd been the man of the house since age four, I'd smoked my first cigarette at seven, and I knew how to assemble and dismantle a Kalashnikov by eleven.

Dad was doing pretty well; he was now a qualified cleric. He taught at the *hawza 'ilmiyya* for 800 tomans a day, and lectured in Arabic Literature at the University of Tehran. But 800 tomans is only about forty cents Australian, so the more things changed, the more they'd stayed the same. We'd moved houses six times in Qom since the war had ended. Nowadays, Mum and Dad, my two brothers and little sister and I were renting someone's basement.

The Mister John Walker

Growing up in a family dominated by Arab speech, my Farsi wasn't anywhere near as good as the other kids', and Dad had an uphill battle finding me a school. At meeting after meeting, schools routinely rejected me, despite my eager recital of a Hafiz poem I knew by heart (not that I had any idea of its meaning).

Eventually, a teacher by the name of Mr Rashidi intervened and took pity on me. He loved Dad's love of the arts and theatre; he loved that Dad was a *different* man of the cloth. Once enrolled, I picked up Farsi in no time.

What's more, I performed in every school play Mr Rashidi had written, and he even had me over for dinner a bunch of times. One night, when his wife had cooked *qormeh sabzi*—a traditional Persian herb stew, absolutely mouth-watering—Mr Rashidi offered me a drag on one of his Marlboros. Mr Rashidi had lost his one and only son during the war, a thirteen-year-old who'd enlisted as a minefield-clearer. He cleared one mine. Perhaps because of this, Mr Rashidi treated me as an adult; he was always happy to discuss complicated politics, and even fantasised openly about what it would be like to stage an uncensored showcase of *Romeo and Juliet* in Iran.

The night he offered me the Marlboro, he must have felt particularly close to me. He started talking about his fondness for liquor.

Before the Ayatollah Khomeini revolution, during the Shah era, he'd tasted what he called the Mister John Walker.

'The Mister Walker is one that plonks you out with happy dreams,' he said, dreamily. 'Dreams of freedom and the smell of air without blood…' There was a glitter in his gaze. 'It's also good for your eyes,' he confided. 'You start seeing your wife in ways you never had before. You'll see the super goggles I'm talking about when you grow up.'

'Does Mister Walker make your wife less older?' I asked. Mr Rashidi's wife was noticeably his senior.

'Yes, Osamah,' he said wistfully. 'It takes a decade off her. And that's only one benefit.'

I sat there, amazed and astonished and feeling important, having been worthy of my teacher's sharing a punishable secret with me. If anyone else had heard such a confession in Iran, he'd have been sacked and imprisoned and, naturally, tortured. I felt an admiration for this rebel of a man, more than any religious authority I'd been brought up to worship. I felt cool, in other words. He puffed cigarette smoke out his nose, and gestured to his pack of Marlboros.

'Osamah, my boy, don't think this stuff's what's gonna kill you. There's a stronger killer, something that suffocates you stronger than the gas. When you grow up, you'll know what I mean,' he said, again, mysteriously.

'Why do I have to learn everything when I grow up?' I asked him. 'Why can't I just know now?'

Mr Rashidi just patted my shaved head, got up and walked into the kitchen, still beaming his signature smile. He kissed his wife on the shoulder and made his way to the fridge. He retrieved a bottle of Mister John Walker, an illegal import, no doubt, walked to the front door, opened it, and stepped out onto the street.

I watched him look over the street, impassively, pour the bottle on himself, shout, 'God is Great!' and then self-immolate. He was flapping as the flames engulfed him, but his wife flapped even harder, helpless and screaming. There was nothing she could do. I just watched Mr Rashidi until he dropped onto the concrete. I read the Koran, silently, to brighten his burned soul.

School crime and punishment

Mr Rashidi was still fresh in his grave when the surviving teachers began to routinely belt the socks off me. Other kids got beaten too, but I was an Arab, and so I had to cop a lot of discipline.

The necessity for discipline made the teachers work hard. The ever-growing need for new and interesting torture techniques opened their imaginations, fuelled their creativities. Instruments ranged from the wooden ruler to the garden hose to the electric cable, applied as needed to the knuckles or the bare soles of the feet. This was not as fun as I am making it out to be. The fun part was walking home if it was snowing; with your feet fresh from the lashings, it was a blessing to be numb. It still stung, but it dulled your pain receptors.

If your hair was long enough that a teacher could grip it in their fingers, it was deemed too long, inspiring them to perform what they dubbed an 'intersection'.

I detested shaved, short hair.

Not from vanity. I'd seen too many dead soldiers on the street, and shaved heads were the one thing they had in common. I always pushed it, growing my hair to three centimetres' length. But you had to be careful: nothing delighted the teachers more than hair long enough to grip and twist between their fingers. Or, almost nothing. They also took special pleasure in the intersections. This involved shaving in a cross-shape, leaving four patches of longer hair, causing strangers by the side of the road to call cruel and droll remarks on your walk home, mainly about watching your step when you crossed the intersection. 'Nice grass patches! Can sheep herd on them?'

The thing about kids is that they're prone to forget things. This is just how kids are built. It's the reason you have to punish them, the reason you have rules, but it's also the reason they'll keep breaking them, over and over, and the reason your punishments can't be uniformly brutal. Like the day I went to school in a short-sleeved shirt.

The day was warmer than usual—beautiful, but hot. I forgot short sleeves were banned, I really just did.

The schoolmaster yelled like a dragon. I saw the fire come out his nose. He called me into his office, saying I needed to be taught to behave. He said I was a no-good, trouble-making Arab. His frog-like lips always made me giggle inside.

He opened up his filing cabinet and pushed me inside. My shoulders touched the edges; my head crammed against the roof.

At recess and lunch I was so hungry, I wanted to ask for my lunchbox, but I didn't dare. He didn't let me out until long after the last bell rang, and everybody else had long ago gone home. I was so scared in that dark box I peed my pants.

Masturbation is a sin

Dad thought I was destined to become a cleric to lead the people, so he'd take me with him to the *hawza* to complete my schooling. It sounds grand, but in practice this meant sitting under the pulpit for endless hours, listening to lectures delivered by the white-bearded imams.

One such lecture, imaginatively titled 'Masturbation Is a Sin', prompted me to join the circle of young men who always gathered afterwards to ask the imam questions.

'What if I have this friend who masturbates but does not reach climax. Is that still a sin?' asked a horny teenager with pimples on his nose.

'Yes, son,' preached the imam. 'Any form of self-pleasure is a sin.'

'What if this person, like my friend, is in bed and he doesn't really know if he's dreaming or awake? Can he keep rubbing against the bed?'

'No, son,' the imam firmly said. 'Unless it is entirely and solely a wet dream, then it is a sin to continue to rub oneself against the mattress or any part of the bed thereof.'

Another boy raised his hand. 'What if a guy I knew inadvertently bumped into a girl at the mall, by *complete* accident, got an erection, and then tried to do the gentlemanly thing by pushing the erection into his pants, using his hand, and in doing so, reached climax?'

You had to hand it to the imams. They always answered questions like these systematically and resourcefully. And although their faces were as wrinkly as old paper bags, it's one of life's great mysteries how they kept straight faces at times like these.

Dad's struggle to keep his cool

While the boys kept up their best attempts to find some religious loophole that would allow them, definitively, to masturbate without guilt, Dad came in and excused me from the imam question time.

'You're too young to sit in these lectures,' he said. To make up for it, he promised to take me to my favourite juice bar, and then to the bookstore, where I'd be allowed to pick any three books of my choice. He also told me he'd enrolled me at the Kanoon Parvaresh Fekri—Iran's leading arts institute—for the fourth year running.

All of this news was uniformly excellent. At the Kanoon, I learned literature and was able to write poetry; I went there to express my rage, and was encouraged to do so. It was more exciting than the illegally imported poster of Pamela Anderson my cousin had shown me under cover of darkness one night, and it definitely gave me a higher high than the imam's masturbation seminars.

We walked towards the rusty gates of the *hawza* to collect Dad's motorbike. Dusk was sneaking down on Qom; the moon had just crept into the sky, getting ready to take over for full-blown night shift. In its low light, we spotted two policemen ordering a tow truck to take away Dad's motorbike. Dad ran towards them, which wasn't easy in full religious garb.

'Lieutenant! Please! I'm here!'

'Cleric, Your Reverence, is this your bike?' an officer asked. You could hear the effort it took to put respect into his voice.

'Yes,' Dad confirmed, shaking both the officers' hands and offering them a tired smile. 'Please don't tow it away.'

'You are Arab?' quizzed the officer. He'd picked up Dad's broken accent.

Dad and I had witnessed this scene many times before. 'I am a citizen of this earth and your fellow brother in humanity,' Dad replied.

'So you are Arab,' said the officer. 'This is a disabled veterans parking zone, *cleric*. You are a man of the cloth and should know it is a sin to take someone else's spot illegally…'

'I *am* a veteran,' Dad responded, taking out an ID card.

'A disabled veteran?' asked the officer. 'You don't seem all that wounded. Unless you're wearing a prosthetic leg under that garb.'

Dad was trying to keep his cool; he was better at it than I was. But he knew how to push his case, when to take a stronger tone. 'Are you suggesting that a person who served eight weeks, got wounded and then never served again is more entitled to this spot than a person who watched thirty-two changes of season on the front line?'

'Of course! He lost a limb!'

'And we lost our minds, lieutenant.'

'How do I even know you were not like those traitor Arabs who played both sides?' the officer muttered. 'Might explain why you left the war unscathed...'

Dad's eye twitched. His lip quivered. For a minute, I thought my stoic, ice-cool father was about to take the policeman's rifle and knock him out with it.

Then he smiled at the officer, and wished him a good day instead. Our plans for juice bars and bookstores were not brought up again; we needed the money to free the motorbike from the police yard.

Looking for Mr X

Today, the snow had coloured the whole city perfect white, and everyone was walking cautiously across the spongy carpet, in mutual agreement to keep all of Qom virgin-white. My cousin Musty and I were walking to the holy shrine, tiptoeing across the thick snow. We were discussing alcohol, naturally.

'When you grow up, do you think you'll try it?' Musty asked.

I considered the question thoroughly. 'Only if I was alone and stranded on an island.'

'That's so stupid,' Musty said. 'Where would you get the alcohol?'

'*You're* stupid! In any other situation Mum and Dad would be nearby.'

Alcohol in Qom was sold in seedy underground markets, usually someone's old war bunker. I was the son of a cleric, my cousin was the son of a cleric and another set of cousins had been born into another family of clerics. In other words, access to these merchants was out of the question.

We had heard about a Mr X, which was bizarre, seeing as the letter X does not exist in the Persian alphabet. He ran a legitimate business near the shrine selling pictures of the Ayatollah, which was as profitable in a place like Qom as fish and chips in London. But he also had a storage space behind the religious photos, where he plied another trade that was more interesting to teenagers.

My cousins and I tried hard to look like ordinary citizens, ones without religious parents. We wore huge silver chains around our necks, thinking these gave us a reckless look. When Musty and I got up the courage to walk into Mr X's shop, we amplified our thuggishness by undoing the top buttons of our shirts, straw hanging out the sides of our mouths like regular John Waynes.

'How can I help you young boys?' said Mr X.

'Are you Mr X?' I asked, suddenly unsure. He was a bearded old man in a *kofia* hat.

'I don't know about this X thing,' he said, 'but I highly recommend this new photo of the Ayatollah. He's overlooking a nature strip. Very colourful, sure to bring a zing to your decor.'

Musty jumped in. 'We want the Mr Walker.'

'What do you think of the Ayatollah?' asked Mr X.

'He's, uh...' I searched for a response. A trap, as usual. If I said I loved the Ayatollah, it would prove I had religious affiliations and expose our thuggy costumes as a terrible front. If I said I hated the Ayatollah, he could hand us to the authorities for a lengthy punishment.

'Get out of my shop,' concluded Mr X, gesturing to the exit with as much force and finality as a cricket umpire.

A real thug would've known how to respond to this scenario. As for me and Musty, we never learned the correct response. We tried schemes like this one time and time again, with various alcohol vendors—there were many men like Mr X. But they always chose not to deal with such unconvincing clients, who could always be gathering intel for the Piety Police. The punishment for selling alcohol was either jail or death.

Beware the Monkerat

Calling them the 'Piety Police' may sound like a diminutive term, but there was a Persian proverb that duly applied to these people: 'Don't scoff at chilli, so puny and small—gorge a handful and your balls will fall.'

They were better known as the Monkerat, which literally means 'against vice'. They worked undercover, and had a talent for smashing people's teeth—in or out, it was up to them. They landed precise punches.

They were different to regular police. They only executed religious warrants. Beardless men were slapped around, as were young ladies who left the house with but a strand of hair poking out from under their hijabs. As for beardless men like me who tried to chat up girls like these? We made the perfect public punching bags for the Monkerat.

The Monkerat shaved their beards to blend in with the sinners. They popped their top two shirt buttons, wore silver chains like me. They slicked back their hair and hung around noteworthy hotspots of sin. They chewed gum far too indolently, spat on the sidewalk to look 'hard'. They even used their prayer beads like genuine street rats did, spinning them in circles round their index fingers while they smoked cigarettes hands-free.

They were very good at what they did, always three moves ahead. Of course, we all spent countless hours trying to make them. We analysed gum-chewing techniques, comparing the styles of thugs to those of the average man on the street: thugs chewed like camels, while the average person chewed gum like a cow. A novice Monkerat would ham his chewing and show too much tongue. But that was when they were novices; they got real good, real quick.

They also spat their phlegm differently. A real spitter with no agenda wouldn't care where their chunky throat soup might land; a rookie Monkerat would hesitate, look around, lest he accidentally dirty a freshly painted wall.

Following this logic, I one day saw a thug spit on a wall that had a slogan from the Ayatollah sprawled across it in official font. A Monkerat would never go as far as blasphemy—that would be like a cop taking real heroin, which doesn't happen, most of the time. I sauntered up to him to get the goss about an alcohol vendor.

'Sup,' I said, bouncing up and down like a gangster.

'Fuck off,' the thug replied.

'Take it easy, bro,' I said.

'You with the pigs? They send you?' He looked me up and down. Lately, the Monkerat had been hiring kids younger than me.

'No, swear to God.'

'Swear on your father's eyes,' he said. 'Say, "May he go blind if I'm lying."'

'May my dad go blind if I'm a cop rat,' I said solemnly. 'Now can you please tell me who's selling some liquid around here?'

'What sorta liquid?'

'You know. Get high.'

'Alcohol?' he said.

My face turned pale. A real thug would never use that word. I inspected his attire again, as casually as I could, trying to pick out a glitch, and suddenly there it was: he was wearing black business socks beneath his basketball shoes.

I shook my head and addressed him formally. I was very close to having a very real problem. 'What alcohol?' I spat. 'Damn you and your evil mind! This is the Islamic Republic! If I *ever* catch you loitering here again, I'll report you to the Monkerat! Be gone!'

A real thug would have belted me. The Monkerat just froze.

It was no use trying to spot them most of the time; they were chameleons. They had a cloak of invisibility unique around the world, thicker and blanker than any other police I've ever seen. That was what happened when you took your job this seriously.

In the end, all we could do was dutifully grow our beards. But we were young, and our faces ended up looking as patchy as KFC chicken wings.

Selling rockets to buy a smoothie

It sucked being cold in winter, and it sucked being in school. But when summer engulfed the city, and we went on break from school, it still sucked being poor. It always did. I wanted to buy an ice-cream, but I was dreaming even bigger. I wanted to buy a cool, luxurious smoothie.

And this was why I moved into a lucrative new business: the provision and sale of fireworks, both legal and illegal. I recruited my cousins and Moe Greene.

We knew of a few Afghan boys who smuggled fireworks across the border, so I negotiated with them to get some merchandise on credit. I had to swear on my mother's eyes that I would not rat them out to the cops and then swear on my mother's womb that I would pay them back.

After consulting with my cousins, we decided to give our goods peculiar names, to find a point of difference and ensure a wildfire word-of-mouth campaign. We stocked the Hitler 1000 rocket—small and Russian-made—and the Genghis Khan, a Chinese-made missile that packed a bigger punch. Our other bestsellers included the Attila the Hun 441, the Pharaoh 2000 BC, and the God's Fury 3000. Each name had its internal logic, sometimes multiple layers. The Pharaoh was Egyptian-made, but it also concealed a rocket within a rocket—inside a tomb, if you will. Better yet, the inner shell generally detonated a while after the initial rocket had popped. Just like a real Pharaoh, it was built to be resurrected. We also sold a Bin Laden for the right fee.

We decided not to cater for weddings or birthdays, or the ever-popular return-of-POW celebrations. It was important not to sell our rockets to just anyone, because (a) they could be Monkerat, and (b) if they didn't know how to set the rockets off, the explosions could be fierce. It was a fast way to get yourself comfy one-bedroom lodgings at the local hospital.

The return-of-POW celebrations were particularly tempting: scores of POWs were trickling back into the country, so we knew that we could make a lot of dough. But one day, we'd sold some rockets to the excited child of one of these returning war heroes. The boy had set off the thunderous fireworks upon his dad's return—and the father, upon hearing the ear-splitting blasts, was forced into nightmarish flashbacks of his days on the front lines. He completely lost his mind, right there and then. He stripped off his boots and fatigues in front of the entire neighbourhood, and ran through the streets of Qom wearing nothing but his socks and a freshly stained set of underpants.

It was a volatile business. Like certain alcohol vendors, our base of operations had to be constantly on the move. We eventually settled at the foothills of the mountains, which had a huge geographical advantage. We knew the landscape well, and there was a low possibility of ambush. We bought two-way radios and tuned them to the police band. One of us would climb the mountain—a full half-kilometre—where he could get a good view of the police. In the event of a police raid, he'd send an emergency signal, a mirror-flash from our comrade at the peak.

Every Friday, we smoked cigarettes atop Prophet Khezr Mountain, tucked inside the small worship cabin, which was built from logs and rocks. Legend had it that the Prophet Khezr, born a thousand years before Christ, had passed through this mountain, built the chapel as a place of prayer, and then vanished, by act of God. The ancient sanctuary was a deeply spiritual place. It was also the perfect stash-spot for our illegal fireworks.

'Sami-Sami-Musty,' I radioed up the mountain.

'Come in, Sami, over,' Musty replied.

'The plain clear, over?'

'Clear as plastic, over.'

'Double-check, over.'

'Shit, I think I see cops. Over.'

For the most part, we aborted missions purely from paranoia—which was still better than getting too comfortable.

The whole job was arduous, and sneaking around only made it more so. We'd instruct buyers to leave their money by a certain cave, and direct them to another cave, where their product was stored. Some buyers ripped us off by depositing fake money. One of them threw in a note that read, *Go fuck yourself*.

'This guy's written *go suck twelve dicks*,' I complained, more incredulous than frustrated. '*Why?*'

'Who cares about the twelve dicks. He's stolen the stuff,' spat Musty.

'Yeah, but why twelve? Why not seven or three or a thousand?'

'Shut up, Osamah! We're losing money here. We have to think.'

We all thought for a solid sunset, smoking quietly at the peak.

'How about we pull off the *Persian* instruction sets from the packaging?' I suggested. 'Leave the Chinese ones on. That way people have to call us to learn how to set the fireworks off.' I got excited. 'Maybe they leave their phone number alongside their payment. And we can call them and give them the details on how to launch the rockets.'

It worked a treat. People still stole our goods sometimes, but they also became walking billboards about the dangers of handling fireworks when you didn't really know how.

It was still a taxing business, and it lasted no more than that unforgettable summer—unforgettable, and grim. There was no way we could have known the group of teenage buyers was the Monkerat—because they weren't really the Monkerat, they were only their conscripts. The boys looked street-hard, and *were* street-hard. They were honest-to-God juvies who'd signed a deal with the District Court in exchange for early release.

The police tracked our payphones and rained down with brutal force. They deposited us in a cell and bashed us to their liking. We gave a sworn statement that we would all be good boys from then on.

When our parents came to pick us up, they gave us such a flogging that at one stage I moaned, 'I just want to go back to jail.'

Dad goes to the Kangaroo Continent

I was man of the house again—only this time, my father hadn't gone out to the front line. He'd gone to a country called Australia to lecture, and to preach, which Mum thought was more dangerous than the war. He'd gone there before, but only for four-week periods, during a special religious month in the Muslim calendar. This time, he'd been called there for a three-month stretch, so I'd switched to a less-risky method of making cash: I was a legitimate shoe-shiner, just outside the shrine. It wasn't exactly smoothie money, but it was enough for books.

I knew that Dad was in for a lot of kangaroos. (We'd watched a dubbed version of *Skippy* on TV.) I also knew there was a Queen who liked colourful hats for obscure reasons. I learned more at the library: it was a country *and* a continent. Its white people wore cowboy hats and raised sheep, while its indigenous people roamed nude and hunted the white people with boomerangs, in retaliation for the white people's having hunted them with bullets.

In one journal I came across the Sydney Opera House: 'that asinine building dubbed the house of the opera which looks like a hideous cockscomb…' Another article emphasised the newness of the country, and placed great import on the population's origins as British convicts. Another told how Australia had never been through a *real* civil conflict, and how its entire population didn't match that of Iran's capital. The articles treated Australia with brevity and contempt. A Kangaroo Continent, impossibly distant from the rest of the known world.

And Dad had gone to this strange, impractical land to lecture its people on Islamic History and Arabic Literature.

He called international every day to see how we were doing, and to check that I was taking care of the house. He was also making real money, and promised that when he got home, we'd finally get to move into a house with actual bedrooms.

He told us about the place he was staying in, which was called Sydney. He didn't mention the Opera House or the beaches. Instead, he was entranced by the abundant aisles of the supermarkets. He understood his audience: we, too, were amazed.

'A thousand different types of cheese?' I asked, flabbergasted.

'A whole aisle dedicated to cheese! They have everything.'

'What about butter?'

'A thousand types of butter, too. And you don't even have to have cheese and butter for breakfast, because they have cereals for breakfast, a thousand types!'

This was clearly ridiculous. During and after the war, we'd been on rations. Each family had received a coupon, entitling them to the basics: vegetable oil, sugar, flour and rice. You could always buy more commodities on the black market, but that was for wealthy families. Prices had been severely jacked up.

In Iran, there are six or seven different types of bread, each unique and 'baked on the spot' at its own special bakery. But the problem of a small town like Qom's being flooded with a population more often found in a capital city was that bread ran out before even half of us got a turn. As such, it was essential to line up as early as 4 am, well before the dawn prayer. Unfortunately, the same situation applied to buying milk, and it was my job to secure both necessities.

It was a daily catch-22. Did I line up for milk for an hour, or did I risk the milk and go for the bread first? The stress had been immense back when I was six or seven. I'd got used to it by now. Practice makes perfect.

My head was spinning as Dad went through his absurd list of products. There was:

LOW-FAT MILK
NO-FAT MILK
FAT-BOOSTED MILK
SOY MILK
GRASS MILK
VEGAN MILK
SMART MILK
INTELLIGENT MILK
STUPID-PEOPLE MILK

LACTOSE-FREE MILK
LACTOSE-ENHANCED MILK
CELEBRITY MILK
WOMEN-ONLY MILK.

We didn't believe him, but he promised photographs.

I wanted to go there. Not really to flee persecution; the truth is, I didn't know any better, it was just our everyday reality. And while I knew about the beaches, I couldn't even imagine them. I didn't dare imagine them—surely such a beautiful location, filled with equally gorgeous women, existed but in heaven. I could barely picture what women looked like without their headscarves. Combine that with the descriptions of Australia I'd read in the library, and you can see why bread and milk were so alluring. Dad also assured us there were no midnight raids by naked tribesmen.

From the questionable reading I'd been doing in the library, plus Dad's stories—he always talked until his credit ran out—I had more than enough ammunition to start bragging. I spent my days telling total strangers how Dad was guiding Christian convicts to Islam, and hunting his breakfast via boomerang.

Many years later, I came to appreciate the absurdity of my impressions. Then again, I was recently asked by a sincere young Australian whether we'd discovered cars yet in Iran or if we still rode on camels, so maybe every teenage boy is short on wisdom.

SIPPING TEA WITH SUGAR

Mashhad, Iran, 2013: five days until visa expires

I've been in the court for three and a half hours, clutching a number in my hand. It's close to 10 am, but nothing is close to happening. I go through a long mental checklist called What I Could Have Achieved in Three Hours. Two soccer games. A few overs of cricket. Disco dancing. A prayer marathon. Queueing up at Centrelink.

Finally, they call my number. I approach the desk. I brief a skinny man with a bushy moustache about my situation. He takes the letter from the police and, without a single word, stamps it.

Back to the coroner's—where I barge my way to the front of the queue. I head straight for the man who dealt with me yesterday, twice.

He looks at me. 'Back in line.'

'Sir, I am under an enormous time constraint,' I plead. I wave the court papers. He remembers me.

'It's close to midday,' he says. 'I told you to go to the courts early. Where have you been all morning? Sleeping in, I bet.'

'Sir, please.'

'Line up like everyone else! You don't get a free pass just because you're *Australian*.'

So I line up, at the end of my nerve. And another two hours pass, just like that. It's not like there's a thousand people here. It's just a bad time of day. Midday in Iran is a triple-threat: it's close to the lunchbreak and the afternoon prayer *and* the afternoon siesta. Not strictly in that order. The man I've been dealing with disappeared a good ninety minutes ago. At 2.40 pm, he returns and calls me. He takes away my papers and promptly issues one more.

'Body's yours,' he says.

'Excuse me?'

'You can take it wherever. I would suggest you bury him here, in holy ground. But it's up to you.'

I'm floored, but still confused. What am I meant to do with the body? 'Sir, what's the process?' I ask him. 'How do I get him to Australia?'

'They didn't tell you that in court?'

'No.'

'If you weren't so slack this morning, you would've been able to do this earlier. In any case—go to the registrar, pay the fee, and ask to have the body transported. To the Paradise of Reza.'

'What's the Paradise of Reza?'

'It's a cemetery.'

'But I want to take him to Australia.'

'Just wait! Stop interrupting! Is this how they culture you over there? It's also a morgue. You can keep the body there until the Department of Foreign Affairs gives you an exit.'

I think about this. 'So Paradise of Reza, then I go to Foreign Affairs?'

I keep finding new ways to disappoint this person, I can see it on his face. 'You need to contact your embassy. Have you done that?'

'Not yet.'

'Then what have you done? You are very slack, I have to tell you. Get a letter from your embassy to say they're happy to accept the corpse back in Australia. Then go to the Department of Deaths and Births and submit your papers from the morgue. They'll issue you a paper.'

'What paper?'

'To take to Foreign Affairs.'

Right. 'Would this be all?'

'I think so,' he says. 'Although, then there's the airline ticket.' It takes me a minute: he means for my dad. 'But you can't buy a ticket until you sort out all your paperwork.'

I thank him. He doesn't reply. Like all the Iranian officials I've met, he takes a sugar cube, dunks it in his tea and gets on with sipping it. I walk away, going over everything I've yet to deal with. As I do, the man calls after me.

'May he rest in peace, son.'

◆ ◆ ◆

The hearse driver, a portly, kind-eyed man wearing thick glasses, tells me not to worry, as the Paradise of Reza doesn't close till 7 pm. I check the time: four-thirty. We've been on the road a good half-hour and the cemetery is still another forty minutes out. The driver tries to make chitchat about Australia. He asks me how much the West hates Iran, and why. I answer in short statements but he is keen to learn more about the 'white folk', and he keeps his questions coming at a steady pace.

Reza's Paradise is enormous. It goes on for miles and miles. The driver instructs me to follow the 'yellow line'; if the situation had left me with any sense of humour, I'd mention something now about the Wizard of Oz.

The body is unloaded and the driver goes, thanking me for all I've told him about employment rates back home (though I was fuzzy on the specifics for the hearse-driver industry, so I couldn't help but disappoint him).

If there is such a thing as the smell of death, then this is it, right here. Dozens of corpses, laid on trays, zipped up in black bags. Dad's is zipped imperfectly, and his hair is visible. Somehow, the hair looks alive. I can't believe he's gone.

I stand there, lost, a few minutes before somebody informs me to register my entry, and to follow a green line. It takes me to a small office where a number of young men are warming themselves over a fire. The main office is far, they say; a bus comes every half-hour. I pay the entry fee, and some extra 'thank-you' money just in case I'll need their help later on.

Back in the room of bodies, wailing women mourn the deaths of their husbands, sons or fathers. They gather to one side as the men of the family lift the bodies off the trays and take them away for the washing ritual.

I help some men lift their loved one and carry him away, chanting prayers with them as we go. When the body is lowered I kneel with everyone, place my right arm over the body and read the *Fatiha*—the first *sura*, or chapter, in the Koran.

The *Fatiha* is the Koran's utility; it performs many roles. It forms a fundamental part of the daily prayers, read a total of ten times a day. But it's also read in the event of death, to 'brighten the souls' of the departed, and funeral rituals are in fact called the *Fatiha*, so when someone passes away a *Fatiha* is organised. Last but not least, it's also used in engagements—when a couple is engaged, people all around them will read the *Fatiha*.

I read it for a few bodies—one youngster, just twenty-two. His face is visible, but unrecognisable, just ash black. The uncle tells me he was secretly engaged to a lover, a city girl from Tehran; the boy was from Mashhad. His parents found out and banished him. He got a job in Kish—an island in the Persian Gulf—so they decided to elope. He took a friend's car, drove to Tehran, close to twelve hours' driving, and picked up his beloved. While he was there he decided to come back to Mashhad, to say goodbye to his parents, and called them from the highway. An hour later, both sets of parents were informed the car had flipped, 200 kilometres from Mashhad. The bride's body was over by the women's section.

I tell the uncle why I'm here, and that I'm alone in Mashhad. Immediately he yells for a group of men to help. They all respond at once, taking Dad's body to the wash hall. They all kneel down and pray for his soul as well. As a group of strangers read the *Fatiha* for Dad, I look at my watch yet again. I wonder about each and every one of my friends and family, again. Where are they now? Are they laughing? Having a good time? Crying? Sleeping? Having sex?

I miss the bus, and ask someone how far the office is. A few minutes by car—so maybe six, seven kilometres. I hit the yellow line on foot. It's a thirty-minute run; the next bus passes me just as I cross the finish line. Deep down, I know I needed the movement for my sanity. Waiting for the bus would've damaged me much more.

The office has sludge-green walls. As usual, photographs of the Ayatollahs salute the visitors.

A woman listens to my story with a rude look in her eye. She mutters they will store my father's body for a fee until I have the Foreign Affairs papers. She asks for my passport, as it's policy to keep government-issued ID. But it's the only identification I have in Iran, and I'll need it if I'm to fly to Tehran. Maybe they can photocopy it, I suggest, so they know it's not a fake.

'Policy is policy,' she says.

I take a deep breath, and explain again, as best I can. I'm all too aware they close in an hour's time, and I don't know what will happen to my father's body if I can't deposit it here. 'It's unreasonable, what you're asking. I need my ID to do all these things. But I also don't want my dad to be tossed out in the cold all night.'

'It's not like he feels anything,' she says.

'Ma'am. What if this was your dad?'

She looks at me levelly. 'I would leave my ID.'

'Miss, if you came to Australia and had this exact same problem, I promise you with all my heart they would look after you very differently.'

'Is this the Australia that is making videos about how their government turns away poor people who arrive on boats from Iran?'

I have nothing to say to her. I try to practise my Zen. I wonder if this woman's always had it in for me, if the minute she saw my Australian passport it was all over. My mouth is cotton-dry, but there's more talking to do. I ask if I can talk to the manager.

He is more sympathetic, but offers little help.

'I want to speak to *your* manager,' I say.

It's too late to call anyone higher. 'Also, there's no one higher than me.' But I think he knows I mean the lawmakers. Suddenly, an idea occurs to me. I do have a card, with my photo on it, back at the hotel.

But going there and back will take three hours.

The manager convinces me to leave my passport here, and to come back and swap the IDs in the morning.

It's not ideal but, then again, I'm running out of options. I take the bus out to Mashhad.

◆ ◆ ◆

I arrive at the hotel at 9.30 pm. I can feel I am no longer welcome.

I ask to use the hotel's phone—a local call, I assure them. I ask the airline when the next flight out to Tehran might be.

'Sir, it's a meat market on every airline right through to next week.'

I take a deep breath. 'Next week?' I say.

'Sir, there are millions of pilgrims who've booked way in advance. Your best bet will be the bus.'

The bus will take twelve hours—meaning I'll lose all tomorrow, spend Wednesday in Tehran, spend Thursday bussing back, and since Friday is the 'weekend' here—it's nothing but catastrophe. I still have three departments left to satisfy.

And I really have to call my mother.

Before I can hang up, the operator saves my life. 'Would you fly chartered?' she says. 'It's very expensive, and if you don't mind the turbulence…'

'Yes, yes, yes!' I cry.

'Okay. Can you get to the airport by ten-thirty tonight? Flight leaves at eleven-fifteen, and if you don't have anything to check in…'

'Fuck it. Let's do it.'

'Excuse me?' she says.

I realise I've said this in English. Thank God. I check the time. I always do. It's 9.42 pm.

'I said let's do it,' I say in Farsi. 'Thank you very much.'

'Alright, so you can pay by credit card. It's four hundred US dollars.'

I want to laugh. Dad and I flew here for about $30, but as I read out the credit card numbers, I pause to kiss the phone. Then I remember that I don't have a passport.

Again, fuck it. We'll deal with it there. I take a taxi to the airport, telling the driver I'll pay him extra if he hurries. He takes the invite like a gentleman and floors it.

At 10.25 pm, I'm handing him a wad of cash. I head straight to the private airline's booth, yelling like a madman that I'm a customer on the eleven-fifteen flight.

I'm met with a beautiful smile—the perks the rich enjoy. I'm so used to being told off after the past few days that I almost double-take when the lady says, 'How can I help you?' She calms me, reassuring me there are still a few minutes left before check-in closes. I take a dozen deep breaths.

She regrets to inform me that my luggage is too much for carry-on, and I'll need to pay a heavy premium. I ask if there's a locker service. No. She directs me to airport management, and asks for my ID. Smoothly, I hand her my card, with photograph.

'What is this, sir?'

'Madam,' I say, 'I fly with this all the time. It's my Australian ID and it's accepted worldwide. Shall I speak to your manager?'

She scrutinises it. Lucky for me, her English is weaker than a decaf latte: the card is my swim pass, valid for twelve sessions. She doesn't dare do anything but issue me a boarding pass. Again, the perks of the rich.

I run to airport management and nutshell the events. The manager, an old man, glass of tea in hand—of course—points me to a corner of his office. 'Drop the bags there,' he whispers. 'Go.'

I shake his hand. I feel like I should hug him.

GIRLS, GIRLS, GIRLS

Qom, Iran, 1995

Temporary marriage

Lecture topics at the *hawza 'ilmiyya* were not limited to masturbation. We also learned about temporary marriage.

This is a Shiite-only concept designed to satisfy the urges of young men without plunging them into the depths of sin. Temporary marriage—*sigha* in Persian—allows a consenting couple to marry each other, under a time lock. When the agreed period is over, the marriage is automatically voided, which saves time, not to mention messy divorce papers.

This was a fascinating world: legal sex.

There were, of course, rules and strictures. A virgin girl would need the permission of a guardian—a forbidding obstacle—and a normal marriage dowry must still be paid. And should the temporary marriage lead to actual intercourse, the girl would have to wait three months before embarking on her next contract.

In practice, this meant virgins were well out of our league. We needed to approach mature women.

In pursuit of such wonders, us boys would often go to the holy shrine under the pretence that we were there to pray. Women were covered head to toe; we could hardly see their faces, let alone make out their shapes beneath the black drapes. So we'd approach a woman at random, gently grab her long hijab and whisper: 'Excuse me, miss, would you like some temporary marriage?'

The response was often, 'Go away, I'm sixty-eight years old.'

Unfazed, we'd move straight on to the next-closest woman. 'How about you, miss? Would you like some?'

Temporary marriage could last anywhere from thirty minutes to a lifetime. It was used by many honest men to get to know a girl—sinlessly, and legally, before they would commit.

Some imams, however, exploited this religious loophole to establish and run underground brothels. It made almost perverse sense: with the dowry rule, the women needed to be compensated anyway. Clerics had the perfect cover. Their line of work allowed them to converse with women openly, and no one would think twice.

They also held lectures at the local mosques divided by gender, and had exclusive access behind closed doors. It was easy to see how some clerics took advantage, effectively becoming an imam version of a pimp. They'd sit behind a large desk, covered with Koranic verses, and humbly offer their services as a 'marriage celebrant'. A selection of temporary wives was just behind the other door.

It was a legitimate practice only to a point. The three-month waiting period between marriages meant there was no possible way that any cleric had enough girls to satisfy demand. The Monkerat ran undercover operations, but they rarely led to arrests. They presumably enjoyed these operations quite a lot.

We stayed away from these seedy places, not because we were afraid of getting caught, but simply because, for all our bluster, we were afraid of real sex and the guilt we knew would come crashing down on us. We could ask scores of women at the shrine for temporary marriage; we always knew their answer would be no. What would we have done if some woman had turned around and consented? I really had no idea; I still don't.

One solitary occasion, without the protection of my friends, I pulled on the hijab of a young woman in her twenties and popped the question, as I always did. She turned around, smiling, and whispered: 'And if I said yes, little boy, what would you do to me?'

I stared at her like a stunned piece of taxidermy for what felt like eternity. Then I bolted as fast as I could out of the courtyard.

Chatting up chicks on top of the mountain

Beyond the fantastical loophole of temporary marriages, girls were vexing. They were distracting and satisfying, a happy-crazy drug. They were hypnotic and impossible, always just out of reach.

The barbershop was a blessing and a curse. It was the only place that could legally display pictures of Western women—and thankfully, because school required us to keep our hair so short, getting haircuts was as common as going to the shrine.

The catalogues were full of '70s hair models with gorgeous, fiery hair, flowing, tantalising, hijab-free. I would flick through these catalogues while waiting for my turn, and find myself going crazy with all this eyeball-fuel. I would long for the barbers to take ages, cutting other boys' hair and chatting among themselves. It gave me more time to subtly masturbate under the sheets. I know I'm not the only boy who took such drastic measures.

It was impossible to talk to one of these creatures in public, or look at one longer than a few seconds at a time without getting caught by the Piety Police. And Mum was just as watchful as the Monkerat.

A series of diligent strategies had to be meticulously executed. I needed a solid reason to get out of the house, get up the mountain with my cousins, and devise them. As always, the shrine came to my rescue.

'Mum, can we go to the shrine tomorrow?'

'Such a good boy,' she replied. 'But you've been spending so much time at the shrine.'

'Oh.' Shit. 'Have I?'

'What's going on? *Sowmeh*, maybe you should do some study.'

'But Mum, you've always said God comes before anything else.'

'I have never once said that. You're thinking of your father.'

'You say eggplant, I say eggplant,' I replied. This was the Iraqi version of *potato–potarto*.

She relented. 'Okay, you can go. But come back right after your prayers. And make sure you pray for your father, too. Aqdas Khatoon—our neighbour—says they eat human beings in the desert and feed the remains to the kangaroos.'

I was out the door before she knew it, my horny cousins in tow. We caught a bus to the shrine, for due diligence.

It was tradition to kiss the door to the shrine upon entry. We weren't planning to enter, but we kissed the door anyway, and asked the Prophet's granddaughter to forgive us for the lies we'd told, the lies we were telling and the lies we were planning to tell. Then we were off to the mountains, where there were no police or mums, the one and only place where nobody but God could castigate us.

We climbed hastily; winter's days were short, and daylight was essential if you wanted to make it back down in one piece.

In the enclaves we'd once used to store our fireworks, we'd planted other kinds of contraband—survival supplies, canned tuna, firewood, gloves, torches, spare batteries. The snow-covered mountain was one giant refrigerator, perfect for chilling drinks.

It also made the trek vastly more difficult, which was great news for us: it meant we were the only three stooges in Qom crazy enough to be on this exact patch of earth at this exact time in the history of the universe.

Once we reached the temple, we performed our ablutions and our afternoon prayers and got down to our strategic business. I felt reckless—like the mobsters I'd seen in Western movies, going to the woods to discuss a hit. I knew there were no bugs here, no possibility of surveillance. It was only us, the smell of rocky snow, and God—and maybe Prophet Khezr's irate spirit.

I laid out my plan, excited. My cousins responded with silence. I could hear the ants gossiping about our stupidity beneath the rocks.

'I *love* it,' said Musty.

Medhi nodded too.

The only thing left was to climb down and do a test drive.

And that was how we found ourselves standing outside the all-girls school.

We were here to gawk at girls. And maybe even talk to them. First we'd need to find Jack's magic beans and grow some magic balls with them. For now—no talking, just gawking. Maybe not even gawking, if we couldn't get Medhi to shut up. He was worried we'd get caught and deported to Iraq. We wasted a lot of time dealing with Medhi's nervous breakdowns. Our fathers were war heroes, we told him. They'd never send us to Saddam.

The three of us lurked incongruously by the school gates, which were very tall, and blocked our views. But the girls' school was extremely close to Ma'sooma's temple—a spectacular pilgrimage destination, allergic to all sin. The last place the Piety Police would expect three boys to do any gawking. It was the perfect crime.

To complete the look, I went to Hajji's, the local grocer, a tiny shop, pungent with spice. The plan was to hide behind a gigantic newspaper—you know, like they do in the movies.

Hajji knew me. He looked at me with grave suspicion. 'Since when do you buy political tabloids?'

'It's for Dad,' I said.

'But your father buys the *Arabic Times*.'

'Er, yeah, he's improving his Farsi.'

'Hasn't he gone away or something? You know, to that far country?'

'Yeah, he wants me to collect them. Every edition.'

I paid nervously and ran back over to Musty and Medhi. Our itinerary was very simple and very stupid.

1. Huddle outside the school gates.
2. Don sunglasses to hide our eyes.
3. Begin reading the tabloid.
4. Girls, girls, girls.

Underneath their black hijabs, all those masses of fabric, we might be lucky enough to see a strand of hair, or even make eye contact. Whoever achieved this would be known as 'the dude'.

The bell rang, the gates opened—and a swift kick struck my rib cage. We looked like three uncouth perverts to everyone on the street, and the Monkerat responded with lightning speed. One officer punched my face so hard it bent into a shape I hadn't even come across in a mathematics class. He turned me into a walking Picasso piece.

They swept us, quickly, unfussily, into an unmarked sedan and sped us towards the Entezami station. The Entezami were cops too—but of the military variety. They had martial ranks and carried machine guns.

They wore green uniforms, black beards and faces devoid of smiles. When they were through with us, we lay bruised and bloodied in the wet basement of the station. But, crazily enough, we were laughing—we were on the biggest high. We had done it. We were all *the dude*. We weren't virgins anymore.

Before the cops swept in, two girls had just had time to flash us. One had lifted part of her headscarf, pretending to adjust.

'I saw a blonde tip,' Cousin Musty whispered.

'Get out of here! You're a legend!' I screeched back, sweating and pulse racing.

'Yeah,' he said. 'On a scale of one to blonde, she was about 8.5 heaven. She was just like the American girls.'

My mind went back to the street near the holy shrine. I reassembled the scene in my memory.

In my preferred version of events, the wide courtyard was empty. The turban festival had ended, shopkeepers had shut up shop, schoolteachers were on vacation—and there were no Piety Police. Only the larks floated by the gold dome of the shrine.

An angel stood across the road, covered in her hijab. Suddenly, like a caterpillar coming out of its cocoon, she flung open the hijab and exposed so many hair strands I could die a happy young boy, in this cement-smelling basement.

The moment outside the shrine had been just that: a moment. But I painted and repainted it, a languorous mural in my mind.

I was dragged out of the reverie when the cops came for Musty. We hadn't planned this far ahead; we hadn't believed we'd get caught. What if each of us gave a different alibi?

He gave me the lowdown later on:

A fist smashed across his jaw.

'Why were you loitering around a girls' school?' barked the cop.

'I have come from Yazd,' he told them. 'Check my ID. I'm not from this town. I was looking for a boys' school. I got the address mixed up.'

The officer threw Musty out. Now it was Mehdi's turn. Mehdi immediately fell to tears.

'Please don't tell my father. I'm so sorry. Please don't deport me to Iraq. I just wanted to check out the school for my sister, to see if she should enrol next year…'

The cop whacked Mehdi once more for good measure and unceremoniously bundled him out. Before we got a chance to talk, it was my turn.

'And what's your excuse, motherless, two-legged mule?' he asked me.

'My name's Osamah and my mother is still alive, sir.'

This was the wrong answer. Whack. He punched me in the jaw. Strangely, my face filled with an anaesthetic sensation.

I tried again. 'We were there because I had to pick up my sister from school.'

'Are you sure about this?' he asked me.

I sensed I'd misspoken. 'I mean *chaperone* pick up, not rude pick up. That's my sister we're talking about.'

'I see. And what is her name?'

'Um, what?' And finally I broke down, sobbing. 'Sorry, sir. I lied, I have no sister at that school, please forgive me…'

The first punch hadn't made me as numb as I imagined, which I learned firsthand when the officer's fist met my face again. It was decided I had to pay a higher price than my cousins, because I'd initially insisted on the lie. The officer brought me into a separate chamber and began to lift me up by the ear.

I writhed in pain, then blurted: 'Sir! Are you telling me when you were my age, your dick never moved for a girl?'

The Entezami officer stopped, bewildered. Then his face slowly changed. I'd never seen a human angrier—in life, films or cartoons. He howled, and then came down on me with a wrath worthy of scripture. He struck me wherever there was flesh and bone.

The harder he hit me, the more convinced I was that he probably had played with himself a few decades ago. He just couldn't admit it because of his uniform.

Operation Looking for Mr Rezaei

In our conservative society, you were far better off relying on hidden contacts, silent codes—something less ostentatious than hanging around outside a girls' school with a newspaper and dark shades.

For example, if a girl answered her doorbell and was wearing a red top, she was generally mischievous and willing. Armed with this folk wisdom, I devised another plan. I dubbed it Operation Looking for Mr Rezaei.

We had to find a neighbourhood far away from our own home—then simply go around ringing doorbells. If a girl in a red top opened the door, voila! If not, no worries. We'd just move along to the next home.

Rezaei was a popular name, the equivalent of Smith in Australia. For this reason, it was perfect. If, by chance, we asked for a Mr Rezaei and got one, we'd simply say we were looking for a different person—the fat Mr Rezaei, the skinny Mr Rezaei, older, younger, shorter, taller, all depending on the situation.

Girls who didn't wear red tops, we knew, could be smart and dangerous. If they smelled a rat, they could just yell 'Dad! Perverts at the door.' We figured we'd cross this bridge when we came to it. If, on the other hand, a girl answered wearing red? We'd treat that door like it was the Pearly Gates, plunging ahead and asking straight away if she was 'willing and keen'.

I went over the plan for weeks, getting my cousins bold and excited. On game day, I gave a long motivational speech, talking up our chances of success.

We met a lot more men than we'd anticipated.

Moustache after moustache, beard after beard. By the time evening rolled around, we were despondent.

So my cousins lost faith in me. But I was undeterred, and kept Operation Looking for Mr Rezaei flying solo.

Then one night, finally, when I was out door-knocking zealously and alone, a girl with large dark eyes answered, a loose scarf on her head. And to my enchantment, a bright red jumper.

'What do you want?' she asked me, in a matter-of-fact tone.

I was freaked out, but I remembered: plunge ahead. Stick to the plan.

'Are you willing?' I asked, sounding nervous and overeager.

She grinned. Her smile could've melted the snow off the Khezr Mountain.

'My dad's making tea, but yes, I'm up for it,' she replied—so casual, she was even popping gum.

She didn't fix her scarf to make it cover her hair; it danced in waves over her face, making me tickle with excitement. So I extended my arm and offered her my sweaty palm. She grabbed it. We stared at each other for a stolen moment.

Her hand was soft, then it was gone. She smiled again and closed the door. I collapsed, grinning, against the wall of the alley.

I'd made contact, skin to skin. I couldn't wait to tell my cousins. That was all we'd wanted, after all.

Standing there in the alley, I brought my palm up to my nostrils. The girl's hand was still on it; it smelled like cinnamon.

I breathed deeply.

It was a life-giving sensation.

Girl-hunting at the movies

The success of this encounter was the exception to the rule; in general, Operation Looking for Mr Rezaei had a low conversion rate. Nothing for it but to roll out another plan. I did not know whether to call this one Plan C or D or E. Who knew what letter we were at by now?

Cinemas all over the world are closely associated with romantic rendezvous of every kind. Lucky for our souls, my cousins and I lived in Qom, where cinemas were safely partitioned into two halves: Male and Female.

'Okay,' I said to Mehdi and Musty, devising the plan out loud. 'So we hang around outside the cinema on a Friday'—the most popular family day—'and wait to see if there are any parents who've brought girls with them…'

Mehdi looked worried, but Musty was hooked. 'Where is this going, Os?' he asked. 'God willing, you're going to say: we will sit next to the girls and pretend we're part of their family?'

I gaped at him. He'd taken the plan right out of my mouth.

We headed to the cinema and found our marks: a family of five, the parents, a young boy and two girls in their teens.

We loitered a while, knowing we had to get the timing perfect. Entezami officers were on the street, scrutinising us openly. The family joined the queue and just like that, we slipped in behind them: a family plus three hoodlums, or a family of eight? To complete the picture, I sidled up to the father and introduced myself, all friendly.

'We only come to the movies once a month,' I told him chattily. 'Most of our time is spent at the mosque.'

He was an older man, all grey-haired and stiff.

'Too many wayward children out and about these days,' I pressed.

The old man just grumbled.

Well, we didn't need to sell it to him, specifically. We just needed to sell it. And to all outside appearances, I was talking to my father. We couldn't believe it. The plan had worked. The daughters looked at us furtively, eyes twinkling. They were onto us, of course, but so much the better. They didn't mind.

We wandered into the cinema with them, playing it as cool as possible. But there were no Entezami in here.

And we were just about to sit down casually beside the daughters when their father turned around and grabbed me by the collar.

'Listen, son. I'm with the Monkerat, but it's my day off,' he said. 'I want to enjoy the movie, and I don't want my wife and children to see me violent. So consider yourselves lucky and get lost.'

The public execution of a gay man

Not all of the *hawza* lectures were about relations between men and women. Some of them were about relations between men and men. Gay people were not people: this was very clear. One day, I saw one of them hanged in a public courtyard.

The noose was hanging low to the ground, anchored by a crane. The condemned was a young man in his late twenties. He stood there in his spectacles, and a prisoner's uniform. On his face there was a resigned expression.

The Entezami officer read out the charges to the gathering throng—it was a strong crowd, masses and masses of people.

The condemned was tall and lanky, but it was the glasses I couldn't get past. They just weren't something I associated with a homosexual. He spent his time bonking men, not reading like normal people. He didn't need the glasses. And they made him human.

Deep down, I felt the tickling knowledge that he *was* a human, and because he was a human, that he shouldn't die.

He was asked, as was the custom, if he had any last words. He politely asked the officer if he could set his hands free, momentarily, so he could raise them to the heavens and pray.

'God will look upon repentance favourably,' the Entezami officer said, and agreed to the condemned man's request.

Once freed, the condemned man, surrounded by a dozen officers, used his hands to pull his pants down and expose his bottom to the crowd. The officer stood up, unholstered his revolver, and shot a full round into the man's head.

The glasses shattered into his face. Blood fountained from his temple. The snow was crazed with a thousand random splotches, all different shapes and sizes, but all the same dark red.

The astonished crowd was silent, except for the man's mother, whose wailing echoed through the courtyard for eternity. It did not stop, but was soon drowned beneath the wave of religious chanting—the entire crowd, passionate, approving.

A brief atonement

One day, my cousins and I conferred and decided to take an extended break from our corrupt behaviours. For all our rebellious spirit, we felt terrible, even monstrous. We'd taken fun to an aberrant level. We had gone astray.

As the children of clerics, we knew just what our decadence could lead to. Looking at girls' hair, knocking on strangers' doors, infiltrating families at the movies, masturbating at the barbershop…how low would we sink next? Might we actually kiss a girl? God! We needed a time-out to reflect upon our sullied souls, and emerge renewed.

So I spent countless days and nights reading up on Islamic jurisprudence, cloistered at home. I went to the holy shrine and sought forgiveness and repented. I began to visit the graves of the martyrs every Friday, and read the Koran to brighten their souls.

Due to chemical conditions in the adolescent body, this reclusion didn't last beyond two months. I was a Muslim in my heart—but the same heart that felt so Muslim pumped hot blood through my body, rendering me pagan.

I accepted a compromise, deciding that my soul was Muslim but my body was 100 per cent agnostic. It knew nothing of Thou Shalt Not, nor of the Holy Text. All its knowledges were governed by the art of fornication. My soul needed a good dose of repentance. My body needed a good dose of romp.

Accordingly, I closed the Koran, rounded up my cousins, and explained my latest plan—Plan F, G, H, whatever.

Payphone pick-ups

That stubborn desert heat was back. That's why they called it stubborn. The city of Qom had turned into a furnace.

We gathered once more outside the holy shrine—this time beside the payphones, which were segregated, like everything: men on the right, women on the left. All around us, more wholesome kids were cracking eggs on the sidewalk, cooking them on the large, flat stones for fun.

I had now employed the services of my younger brother, Moe Greene, who had started moving up our adolescent ranks. Moe had been a great warrior and comrade of mine since an early age, and was thereby my most trustworthy relation.

Today, he was required to secrete a cache of Bin Laden rockets inside a garbage can across the road. I had carefully choreographed our foursome's movements:

1. Musty chats to the Entezami officers in a distracting fashion.
2. I walk to the women's phone booth and attach an 'out of order' sign I've made.
3. Mehdi keeps watch for a possible Monkerat ambush.
4. Moe detonates the fireworks.
5. Everything works perfectly.

The other thing I needed to do during the chaos was call our home phone number from the *men's* booth, then leave a pen and paper atop the phone.

The idea was this: after all the madness—the out-of-order sign; the explosion across the street—the girls would naturally be forced to use the men's booth. Because I'd already dialled our home phone, any girl who entered would themselves have access to my number on redial.

As soon as a girl approached the booth, I'd line up behind her. This would appear legitimate. It was the men's booth, after all. Safe and confident, I'd lean close to her hijab and whisper, 'Hit redial!' If she was anywhere near as daring, she would do as I'd asked, causing my home phone number to come up on the screen. She would then use the pen and paper I'd provided to write down my number, pocketing it for later use. Mum never picked up the phone, and Dad was in Australia. So when she called back later, I'd be the one picking up the phone.

It was elaborate, but life in Qom called for elaborate measures. If anything, this guaranteed against failure.

Still, I was sweating, badly. I was worried about the sign hidden under my shirt—what if the sweat rendered it illegible?

Musty was already in the shade beneath the minaret, where the Entezami officers liked to park themselves. Mehdi looked about to die from anxiety, and Moe looked so high I could've sworn he'd eaten pure octane for breakfast.

Musty started to natter away. I looked across to Moe. He beamed a smile and headed to the bins, match and lighter in hand. Mehdi signalled a possible Monkerat at my two o'clock; I waited, but then I saw the thug spit at a freshly painted wall, a reasonable sign that he was not an undercover officer.

People walked past us rapidly, busy with their days, all ready to write and wipe the next chapter of their lives and then:

BANG!

The noise of the explosions filled the street. *God bless you, Moe, you truly are the brother of my dreams.* The chaos and the mayhem were too beautiful. There was smoke, there was fire. The street felt under attack. I ran to the phone booth to execute my end of the deal. I saw Moe smiling, resigned to the fact he was about to be belted. His smile widened as the three officers prepared to take him down. He gestured at me—victory!—and his eyes said: *We did it, bro.*

That's when I pulled the plug on the operation.

I could not do it. I couldn't go through with the plan—not when my little bro was about to have his bones cracked in.

I ran to the site of the explosion and drew the officers' attention, abusing them with every name that came into my head.

'Stop it, you dirty donkeys, you hairy camels! Leave him alone! Pick on someone your own size, you two-legged mountain goats!'

They considered my suggestions.

They implemented them in due course.

WE'LL GET THERE WHEN WE GET THERE

Tehran, Iran, 2013: four days until visa expires

The chartered plane gets into Tehran just after midnight. I choose a cabbie without arguing the price and tell him, 'Take me somewhere cheap.'

'How cheap?' he asks me, snapping gum—a driver with an attitude. 'Beetles-on-the-floor cheap, mice-in-the-walls cheap, druggies-fighting-next-door cheap?'

'Not that cheap,' I say wearily.

He drops me at a strip of 24/7 motels. Before he goes, I enquire discreetly about 'the drugs', thinking I could use something to help me stay awake and alert—there's no time to sleep but a handful of hours here and there.

'I've got prescription stuff, mainly. Codeine, Tramadol, Oxy…'

'Oxy's too strong,' I say. 'It's like morphine.'

'It's an opiate! It's good for you, my friend.'

His tramadies are 200,000 tomans for a box of twenty-four. I do some mental arithmetic—$70 Australian. What the fuck am

I doing? I don't need Tramadol. I've never had them before—but I do read, and what I've read is they give you a sustained, relaxing high. He guarantees they're clean, and downs a tablet right in front of me, just to prove his point.

'Truck drivers use this all the time. You'll be as beast as a Mack with one of these.'

I check the time and accept the offer. Worried how the box might look if anybody finds it, I unpack it and stash the strips in my backpack. I hand the box back to the driver. 'God be with you,' he coughs. I find a decent room. It's way past three. My head is a minefield. I see a trio of cockroaches near the bed shake their antennae, perhaps over my purchase, and I fall asleep.

◆ ◆ ◆

Four hours later, I wake up and take a shower. I can't put off telling my family anymore.

I call Moe Greene, my tough younger bro. I ask him to round up the family and put me on speakerphone.

I still dance around it, until Mum gets sick of me. 'Why are you calling?' she says. 'My blood's dried up. Just spit out what's on your mind.'

'Okay,' I say. 'I'll make this quick. There's no easy way to say this, but I think you should read the *Fatiha*. Dad's passed away.'

I hear a loud scream. Then the sound of my sisters crying. I can't bear it.

'Listen, I only have a minute here. I have to go, there's so much to do, but I promise you I will bring him back. I love you all.'

'Please! Wait!' Mum says, in deep agony. 'Tell me he is just sick, in hospital. Tell me he'll be okay.'

'No, Mum. He's been dead for three days.'

More screams, more crying.

'I'm sorry I didn't call earlier. I wanted to have everything in order.' I hang up the phone and head out.

I don't want to think about what my family is going through—it will just slow me down. Luckily, my hunger is drowning out my thoughts. I find a small breakfast joint and order.

❖ ❖ ❖

I call the Australian Embassy. I speak in English—and the lovely lady tells me I can come in anytime.

'Do you mean the young cleric?' she asks. She recognises Dad from his trips back to Iran over the years. He had come and gone to complete his PhDs, publish his books and for pilgrimage over the years—although this trip had come after many years away. I confirm it's him, and tell her I can be there in an hour.

At the gates, I'm met by a guard with a machine gun.

I show him Dad's passport. 'This isn't an Australian passport,' he says. 'And where is yours?'

'Dude, this *is* an Australian passport. I've called them already—'

'They don't give appointments here.'

'So check with them.'

'Show me your passport.'

'My passport is in Mashhad.'

'Why is it in Mashhad? You don't have a Mashhadi accent at all. Are you lying?'

A black car with tinted windows pulls up. An Iranian man opens the door; two Westerners exit. They look 100 per cent Australian: pale white men in suits. Best of all, they're speaking with my accent.

'Mate!' I yell. They look over, but just nod and walk in.

The guard taunts me. 'You are nothing to them.'

I must admit, I don't look my best. My clothes haven't been changed in days. My facial hair's out of control. Maybe I'm insane in thinking people might see me as anything other than a street rat.

I beg the guard to just call in and check if I am lying. I offer him 100,000 in Iranian money—about a week's wage. I place a large banknote in his hands. He checks to see if the note is fake. When he realises it's real, he almost drools. He buzzes in: 'There is an *Arab* to see the ambassador.' I want to strangle him. I call over his shoulder, in English, that I'm an Australian citizen, seeking help for an emergency. The gate buzzes open.

It's a quick affair inside. Dad's passport is taken. The first page is cut with scissors and handed back to me. I'm given instruction on what form the cargo needs to take, instruction on the embalmment process. I'm told to translate important papers using the official services and given a number to call if I need help, even after hours.

I take a taxi to a translator's office, where I'm greeted by a short lady with a slight hunch.

'How fast do you want them done?' she asks, in Farsi.

'I need to be back in Mashhad tonight.'

'What makes you think I'll have time to finish them today?'

'I'll pay extra.'

'Where are you from?'

'I don't know.'

'You don't know? What kind of an answer is that?'

'I'm from here. I grew up in Iran.'

'But your name is Arab.' She examines me from behind her specs.

'I'm an Australian citizen.'

'Do you speak English?'

'Of course.'

'Why don't you translate them yourself?'

'They need to be official.' But I switch to English, to demonstrate. 'What's with you people? Your culture is rich with poets and painters. Full of history and all that's left is a sad, unhelpful bunch in a stinking polluted city, more worried about where my great-grandfather's from than about how you can help me.'

'Wow. Your English is good,' she says. I pause. She smiles.

'Can you do this for me? Please?' I beg. 'If you can read the papers, you can see I lost my dad two days ago.'

'Okay, go. Come back in two hours. Exactly two hours.'

She's as good as her word.

❖ ❖ ❖

I catch a car to Qom, the city of blood and uprising. I still have my belongings in the apartment where we had been staying, and I have to pack up and pay for the stay.

The car arrives at 6 pm—to Qom central, the shrine. I kiss the door and walk into the grand yard. I ablute in the icy water by the fountain and head inside to rest and reflect.

I can't think too much about Dad's death, but I do think about Dad. What he was doing. *How* he was doing. How he is lying among the dead right now, waiting to rest. I ask Imam Reza's sister, Ma'sooma, for help. I tell her I'm not terribly religious, but if she has the power to pull thousands of pilgrims by the hour, then I beg her to send some my way, and push me forward.

My stomach sends me to the toilet to remind me I'm still a human being. I squat inside the cubicle, deep in thought. *Will I ever be able to smile again?* I wonder. *Will I ever go back to telling my jokes?* Almost seraphically, the gent in the cubicle next door lets rip the most feral fart, long and loud and infinite. When he's done, he discharges another short five-second blitz just for good measure. His sounds of joy and anguish as he tries to release are the perfect cover for my schoolboy giggles.

I leave the toilet, thanking God for showing me that life comes down to this. If Yasser Arafat had told a good fart joke when negotiating with the Israelis, he might even have ended up achieving peace.

◆ ◆ ◆

I've packed up, paid the rent and I now wait in the bus terminal, leaving Qom for Mashhad again.

It was due at nine-thirty but it's already 10 pm. I ask him what time he thinks we'll get there. The driver tells me our ETA is eight tomorrow morning, but we've got at least a thousand kilometres to cover.

I call up my memory of *The Castle*. I tell him he's dreaming.

'Can't rush,' he tells me. 'We'll get there when we get there. Maybe we'll have an accident. Maybe we'll never get there. Where's all your anxiety going to go then?'

At 11.20 pm, we finally have departure. Everyone chants a good-luck verse and the tension drops. But not for me.

THE GREAT ESCAPE

Tehran, Iran, 1995

Dreaming of polar bears

'My son has had a dream,' my mother said, with an air of great solemnity.

The war was long over—but here I was again. Dragged into a small, dark tent by my mother, who was once again electing to deal with me via a woman who'd crawled straight out of a classic children's treasury and into modern-day Tehran.

She looked exactly like the fortune teller I'd seen during the war, the one who'd told me I'd grow up to be a therapist. I did not know where all these fortune tellers did their training, but I was certain they must've used the same plastic surgeon: nobody on earth was born looking quite this strange.

'Hmm,' the old witch hummed into my ear. Her weird lips pressed inwards. I was sufficiently creeped out.

'Go on. Tell her,' urged my mum.

'I had a dream we were living in a green place,' I said, 'with lots of polar bears all around us.'

'Hmm,' she continued. 'Tell me, are you planning to travel soon?'

'Aren't you supposed to know that?'

My rejoinder was met by a solid smack on the back of my neck. 'Ow.' But this was a touchy topic for my mother; she had a lot riding on it. We'd been waiting on refugee status for almost two years, ready to join my father down in Australia. Dad had applied for us to get humanitarian visas after his first visit to Australia in 1993, but he didn't tell the family (particularly knowing my big mouth may spread the word and cause trouble). He waited on the news until 1995, when he finally got a preliminary conditional 'yes' and we had to undergo a medical exam. We had been persecuted in Iran as Iraqis for far too long and, knowing our lives were bleak, he had presented our case to give us a better future.

'Your dream is clear,' said the fortune teller. 'You will get your visas. You will live in Australia. And you will become a great doctor.'

Mum was overjoyed. She hugged me and kissed my shaved head a thousand times, thanking the Lord her offspring was finally going to be of some use.

'And since your son will be a great doctor in a faraway land,' the crone went on, 'I will have to charge you an extra success fee.'

Mum was so happy she didn't care. She showered her in money. For my part, I was horrified, thinking this was all well and good, but where would our next meal come from? We were going to need those coins.

As it turned out, she was right and I was wrong on this one. Three weeks later, our application was approved.

I met the news with some sadness. Australia was so far from Iran that it must have been governed by a separate god.

America cannot dare do a damn thing to us

Soon, I was at the airport with my family: Mum, Dad, Moe Greene, Ali, Mona and baby Roah. We were surrounded by customs officials, not to mention their Kalashnikovs.

It was critically important that we did not speak Persian here. We had to speak Arabic, and only Arabic. We were not to be seen as Iranian residents departing for good, but Iraqis who happened to be passing through. (We'd already destroyed our Iranian Green Cards and after lots of hush-hush transactions, Dad had obtained forged Iraqi passports to fly out with.)

Like the rest of the country, the airport was pulsing with undercover agents who were ready to stop us at the slightest provocation. Dad understood the urgency better than anyone; he'd already fled one country—fled from Iraq, to here. We'd heard the story many times. It never got less awful.

I could picture it quite clearly. The thin mattress on the dirty floor of the tiny room in the house that smelled of mud and of cement that never dried. My father reclining, feverishly scanning his sheets of newsprint, reading and flipping, flipping and reading, with all the concentration of a kid cramming for his finals.

It was 1979. Saddam Hussein had just taken power, and only pro-government Iraqi papers were allowed. Dad, with cash he'd earned at his own dad's tailor shop, would exchange dinar for US dollars and then, through a mule, buy the illegal Iranian newspapers every week.

The punishment for anyone caught was, of course, a brief, unfussy death. Nonetheless—his bedroom was already the room of a scholar, with newspapers like this one crammed under his bed. Books were stacked all around him, on the floor, against the walls, shelved against each other; on the wall beside his mattress was a poster, ripped and repaired, of a black-and-white Audrey

Hepburn, with her trademark cigarette, a classic photo unlike any taken by an Iraqi's lens.

Dad was lounging around with two best friends, Arif and Haitham, who also happened to be his newspaper and US dollar suppliers. When they gathered, they talked big about what they'd do to Saddam if they got the chance. But mostly, they just talked about movies. Dad's nickname was 'Hollywood Encyclopedia', an honour bestowed on anyone in Iraq who could name three films starring Stallone and De Niro. He also harboured a theory that De Niro and Pacino were the same person; it was only years later that I finally convinced him to watch *Heat*, at which point he was happy to pass the title down to me.

Everyone had learned to recognise the knocks of the Baathist militia. They were notorious for shooting those suspected of anti-government leanings at point-blank range, feeding their bodies to ravenous dogs, and then invoicing the families for the cost of the ammunition. But that morning, no knock came. They just pushed the door in.

My father ordered his friends to scale the gas pipes and get out; he knew he had to stay with his mother. What could they do but flee? In seconds they were outside, leaping from rooftop to rooftop, the soldiers chasing them with a scatter of bullets.

His mother collapsed at the commander's heel. 'Please, my son is a good boy. Take me instead.'

By way of reply, the commander smashed the butt of his rifle into her face, and ordered my father to kiss his boots. They bundled him into a military jeep and left his mother on the floor, wailing and bleeding.

Later, they stripped him and hung him by his feet from a ceiling fan. They left a steel table spread thick with surgical tools strategically in view.

The interrogator was his uncle. Wartime does strange things.

'Fuck, Sami,' he said. 'You've made my day so difficult. How am I meant to have dinner with your aunt tonight? There won't be peace for days. Just give me your friends' names, and I promise to end this quick.'

He plugged in an iron, like the type his wife used for saner reasons every week, and let it heat.

After fifty-eight days of torture, two soldiers came for him. My father was to be transferred to Abu Ghraib. The warden there, his uncle warned, was not a 'family man' like him. But he was glad to be rid of my father, so that his home life could know peace.

Little did he know these 'soldiers' were Arif and Haitham in costume. Again, war does strange things. They had used the fifty-eight days to grow their moustaches thick enough to fit in, and had crafted replica uniforms with the help of my father's tailor shop.

They drove straight for the border, and crossed into Iran by swimming the shallow marshland. There were no other options.

In 2003, my dad was finally able to call home again. He was told his father had passed away, but his mother still lived. All this time, she'd believed he had been executed.

When my father got off the plane in Basra, to see her for the first time in twenty-four years, he was informed that she'd suffered a heart attack after speaking on the phone with him, and passed away in her sleep.

So Dad understood what it was like to lose your family, and had no interest in doing that again. In the airport, a barely controlled tension buzzed around him.

I, on the other hand, was a twelve-year-old, and I had never once been on an aeroplane. After hiding from aircrafts half my life, stashed into underground bunkers, I could not believe that this was happening.

An announcement crackled through the loudspeaker: 'Mr Rezaei, please make your way to gate four.'

I couldn't help but smile at this. Good old Mr Rezaei had come in so handy for me, so often; whoever he was, I wished him well on his journey. Then my smile dropped, and my stomach flipped. I was leaving *everything*. I wondered whether, in Australia, I'd be able to go around door-knocking, and what it would mean if the door was answered by a girl in a red shirt.

'Can I speak a *bit* of Persian?' I asked Dad. 'Like to say "hi" and "how are you" and things like that?'

'No!' Dad snapped.

'But Dad, even stupid people know how to say hello in the language of the country they're in.'

'Well, you're more stupid than a stupid person. We all have to be.' Our accents were too fluent. As soon as we opened our mouths, the customs officers would know that we had been born here, and our whole cover would be kaput. But I was itching to talk. I loved to talk. And what if an officer greeted me, should I ignore him? Dad had spent years teaching me manners and it would be rude not to reply.

'But Dad—'

'Osamah! You know how you like acting? Just pretend you are a character! Your character doesn't speak Farsi. End of story.'

'Cool!' I replied, as we approached the customs desk. 'So. What is my backstory?'

Dad's eyes widened sharply behind his glasses. 'What backstory?' he exhaled in a single breath.

'When I did theatre in school, I always had to develop a backstory, even for a small character, like the wind. When I'd played the wind, I'd come from a tornado.'

'Your backstory is that twelve years ago, I made a huge mistake by having you,' my father said. 'Now shut up and let's go.'

I stopped right where I stood. He was rarely snappy like this. But, despite the urgency, he stopped too and squatted by my side.

'Son. Don't act. Just be,' he said.

This, I could work with. I loved the idea of just *being*. Doing some of Shakespeare's plays, I'd heard 'to be or not to be', but never had it felt so meaningful.

So we advanced towards the customs desk, my brothers and sisters mute, no backstories necessary. My mother was praying in whispers; deep lines of anxiety spidered her face.

Dad, though, was cool as art. He spread our seven Iraqi passports on the desk like a rainbow's arch.

'Where are you travelling to?' the bearded customs officer barked.

'Sorry, no Persian,' replied my Dad.

'Yeah, Arabic only,' I loudly concurred. Dad barely glanced at me over his shoulder.

'You are going where?' insisted the beard, still in Persian.

'I don't understand your words,' insisted my dad, smiling and waving his hands about.

All at once, I started to giggle uncontrollably. We were pulling a scam, and it was working.

The officer clocked me, scowled, and took our passports into a back room. Everything went still. What was happening? None of us could speak.

I wanted to talk. I wanted to roar. I wanted to whisper.

I wanted to let the world know I was here.

A bunch of soldiers were surrounding us, in the corner. Some of them were pretty young. I tried to breathe normally but for some reason I couldn't. My chest was heavy, like I was in a sealed cube.

Who were we, anyway? Did we really scare the authorities this much? Why did they need to point their guns at us? Dad was tough, but not scary. I was strong, but not that strong. I could probably take one of the guards—if he was tied up. Moe Greene was another story; he could have taken three.

I was itching to move. Everyone was so still. Even passengers had stopped coming in and out of the terminal.

I wondered if lightning was just God's way of breaking tension in the skies. I wondered if earthquakes were just the earthly equivalent.

I knew that if I moved, the guards would spring to action. I had a sudden, undeniable urge to untie and retie my shoes. Surely just one shoe—surely that wouldn't get me killed?

I wondered if it would, though. Dad had told me to be still.

But before I knew it, I was dropping to the ground. I fiddled with my shoelaces.

No shots were fired. Not even a 'freeze or we'll shoot'.

They didn't. Say. Anything. What a disappointing relief. And how strange that fiddling with one's shoes could feel so much like freedom.

Nobody was shooting me. Well, except my family, with their eyes. But they couldn't say anything, any more than I could.

So I untied my shoe, then retied it, at first gingerly, then really going to town. I untied and retied it, over and over again. The guards seemed to be okay with me doing this, for now.

Suddenly, one moved his gun in a 'stop it' gesture. I took the point and stood up and stared at the dull roof.

But the dull roof stayed dull, and I stayed fidgety. When you're twelve, it's hard not to act like it.

I looked over at a banner sprawled across the wall. It said in Persian: *America cannot dare do a damn thing to us.*

It was a famous saying of Ayatollah Khomeini's, which was often found spray-painted on walls all over the country. I wondered about these Americans, and why they wanted to do damn things. I wondered if Australia was anything like them—I wondered if they were the devil too.

I began mimicking the Ayatollah in my head, daring the Americans to try and get us. I raised my hand to the sign, like I was greeting a dictator. A great voice boomed behind me, electrocuting me.

It was the customs officer. He was back, and standing right over me. My heart seized. Shit. How long had he been standing there? How long had *I* been standing there? Had I been mouthing the words?

Why, for once, could I not just *be*?

'You can read our leader's words on that banner?' the beard said carefully.

I just blinked back at him, wondering what I should do.

Then for once, I stopped wondering and went into autopilot mode. I began reciting the Arabic alphabet, which incidentally is exactly the same as its Persian counterpart. They're similar in writing—like English and Italian—but they, of course, are completely different languages.

I continued to blurt the letters in Arabic, showing I could 'read' the banner but certainly could not *understand* the words.

The beard kept gazing at me. He then grabbed my ear and leaned in: 'I know you can understand me…I know it…You're just lucky I can't prove it,' he said in a low voice.

I pulled my eyes away, still reciting.

The beard handed Dad the passports and ushered us to the departure gates.

I looked over at my father. I wondered if he was proud of me.

THANK YOU FOR YOUR COOPERATION

The desert, Iran, 2013: three days until visa expires

By 1 am, the bus has had to do plenty of stopping; we're two hours into our trip and we are still getting nowhere. I take the opportunity to coordinate with my family back home, where my brother tells me the community has been flooding the mosque to do the *Fatiha*, which is held over three successive nights. It's only to be expected—Dad was the cleric there—but still, it warms my heart.

I look out the window to see what the hold-up is, and see that it's just a long queue to fill up on diesel. Are you kidding me? We didn't do this before it left the terminal?

The driver notices my anxiousness. 'Easy, kid,' he calls back. 'Just relax. I told you, we either get there or we don't.'

A passenger in his forties, a cleric, like my dad, puts in his two cents' worth. 'Job, the prophet, was known for his patience,' he begins. I am in absolutely no mood for a parable. Is anyone?

Thirty minutes later, we are on the road to Mashhad again. It's just the bus, the highway, the desolate desert and my thoughts.

My body wants to sleep, is desperate to, but my brain just can't. I wonder if I should pop a Tramadol to help me stay awake, but decide against it for no reason other than an article I read in high school about a girl ODing on a single pill. The best I can hope for, relaxation-wise, is to gaze up at all the stars. Some party they're having up there.

❖ ❖ ❖

'Quick toilet break!' shouts the driver.
It's 3.40 am.
At 4.05 am, we're still waiting for one last man. The driver is yelling out for him into the dark and empty desert, but the empty desert shows no signs of calling back. The cleric to my left, who I have nicknamed Cleric Job, raises a hand to calm me: *It will be okay*.

Just then, a tall, fat man with a decent beard going emerges from the desert with a teacup in his hand. Where the fuck do you find a cup of tea in the desert after midnight? It's flat, lightless plains of sand as far as the eye can see, well beyond the limits of the headlights. Must've gone far for that tea.

'You ass,' I seethe through gritted teeth. 'Hop on the bus before you delay us even further with your utter selfishness.'

Before you could click your fingers, a small gang of bearded men rise up from seats behind me and approach, wielding large kitchen knives. Turns out, the fat man is the leader of a small Kurdish tribe.

The driver tries to calm things, while Cleric Job chants prayers, asking for a divine intervention. All I'm armed with is Dad's walking stick. I lift it like a sword.

'You know who you were talking to?' asks one of the Kurds, swivelling his shiny blade towards my general intestinal zone.

'I don't fucking care!' I yell. It feels good to do this. You can't yell at a bureaucrat, but you can yell at anyone who's pointing a knife at you, as it tends to invite a response. 'It was a toilet break, not a jerk break.'

'We're fucking Kurds!' he shouts, moving up the bus. 'You don't mess with us!'

Cleric Job stands in the middle, requesting patience from both sides. But I have turned into a mad beast. I bellow from the pits of my belly. 'I'm crazier than you, fucker! I'm half-Kurd, half-Iraqi, half-Iranian, half-Aussie, half-animal! My dad's sitting in a fridge in some morgue in this fucking country, I have to be out of this damn place in three days and I don't have shit! You want to stab me? Go right ahead, but I'll fucking stand here and take you all down with me!'

Silence falls across the bus, a blanket that settles, soft and slow. The Kurds stare at me from under it, eyes glinting like their knives. I breathe in oxygen and breathe out rage: you can see it. You can sense that I'm not bluffing.

Cleric Job begins to chant a religious prayer. A few other stunned passengers follow. And then the Kurds back off.

'I am sorry for your father's loss,' Cleric Job tells me. 'Like the story of Job—'

'Fuck Job,' I snap back, thankfully in English. I then switch to Farsi, which has the added bonus of calming my shit down. 'Thanks, cleric, for your words. I know of tests and patience. I always preach about life's beauties and brutalities myself, but I'm only human. And I have a thousand things to do.'

◆ ◆ ◆

The bus stops again an hour later. It's still very dark outside—an endless desert, endless dark, except the endless stars. Before I have time to make known my disappointment at the hold-up, a pride of soldiers storms the bus, barking garbled instructions.

I'm sitting right at the front, the first one under fire.

'ID!' he yells.

I withdraw my swim pass and show it to the soldier.

He looks at it with righteous rage. 'What's this?' he shouts, 'What's this?' waving the card back at me.

I start yelling back in English.

The soldier points his gun at me and instructs me to disembark. I pretend I don't understand him. The English words keep spurting out.

'We have an illegal on this bus,' I can hear the soldiers calling back out to their colleagues, spreading it further down the bus.

I want to believe that this cannot be happening, but the machine guns and the yelling men are doing their best to make it absolutely clear that this is the real deal. It's not just a hazy, all-night bus ride anymore, drifting in and out of peace, gazing blearily at the stars. *Things like this* can happen, and now it really is. By the time they find out my passport really is in the cemetery, by the time they cross-check, by the time I'm out of jail, it will be way beyond too late to get my dad's body back home.

While the other soldiers sweep the bus, shaking people down for their IDs and looking through their bags for trafficked contraband, the commander handles me personally.

'What's this?' he barks, pointing at my guitar.

Again, I pretend I don't understand, making a point of gesturing—please—not to be rough with it. I want to come up with a backstory for my character who can't speak Farsi, but I'm only thinking survival, so I just bite my tongue.

'And what's *this*?' asks a soldier quietly.

He's found the Tramadol strips.

'Drugs?' he says in Persian.

I have to step carefully.

'Panadol. Do you know? Headache. Panadol. For headache.' I point to my head, wincing to mimic pain. If anyone here can read English, I am fucked.

'Where is your passport? Passport? Do you know what I am saying? Passport?' the commander shouts. All over the world, there are certain people who believe that you'll suddenly speak their language if they only yell it at you loudly enough times.

I reward this theory. 'Yes! Yes! Passport! In hotel! You know? Hotel!' I thank heavens the words for 'passport' and 'hotel' are the same in both English and Farsi—and that the soldiers seem to believe I can't understand their conversation.

One soldier, to his commander, in Farsi: 'He looks Arab. I think he's having us on.'

The commander: 'No Arab can talk English that good.'

He turns to me, and in a cracked accent asks, 'Hotel? You, where?'

'Mashhad. Hotel in Mashhad. Passport in hotel.'

'Your passport is in a Mashhad hotel? Maybe you come back with us to the station and we make some calls,' he says in Farsi, his English clearly running out of fuel.

I'm not meant to have understood these words, but they'd sound bad in any language. 'No,' I start to protest. Then the hand of God comes in.

'Excuse me, sergeant,' says Cleric Job. 'He is from Australia.'

'Sorry, Sheikh, but do you speak English?'

'No, but you're right, he is an Arab, and I speak Arabic. And those were headache tablets you found in his backpack; he's had a tough time with that since getting on this bus. I think everyone here will tell you the same.'

The commander looks over his head, towards the back of the bus. To my surprise, the Kurds stand in unison and echo the cleric's words.

I am overwhelmed with feeling. I don't know what to say. I take out my iPhone, switch it on and flip wildly through the photos, showing the commander every pic I can, pushing my case beyond reasonable doubt.

'See? Sydney Opera House.' Flip. 'See? MCG, a stadium in Australia…'

'Can you ask him if he was at the Iran–Australia soccer match in 1997? The one where we beat them to qualify for the World Cup?' The officer asks the cleric.

I soon find out Cleric Job's Arabic is as rusty as my first Datsun. I nod my head, yes.

The soldier smiles. 'Iran good football. Australia not very good football.' He hands back my swim pass, the Tramadol strips, the guitar. 'Thank you for your cooperation,' he says. With that, the soldiers vanish.

I don't know what to say to the cleric, let alone the Kurds, who have gone back to their mysterious business at the dark rear of the vehicle. We all just want to get to Mashhad, sure, but none of us signed a contract saying they'd turn back the bus if we weren't all delivered in one piece—they didn't have to help me.

'Thank you for your cooperation,' I whisper to the glass. The desert is slowly brightening, but there are no signs of the soldiers' truck. People are falling back to sleep, as if it never happened at all.

CULTURE SHOCK

Melbourne, Australia, 10 August 1995

Kangaroo Continent

One minute I was on my very first plane ride, thrilled and tired, jetting across the continent in a cool tube of aluminium.

The next minute we landed, and everything was wrong. People swarmed around us, speaking gibberish. The announcements were in gibberish, only from an official source. Stuck to the walls and ceilings, the signs were gibberish too—except the luggage sign, which was a picture of a bag.

I grabbed on to the image and clung for dear life. It was the only thing I knew here. That, and my family.

'Dad, look at that woman. She looks like a man.'

I meant that she was wearing jeans.

'Here isn't Qom, son,' Dad said.

'So why is Mum still covered up?'

Dad shrugged. 'Ask her.'

There was no chance my mother would be removing her long abaya just now. She gritted her teeth and stared ahead and moved through the surging crowd. She was openly terrified.

CULTURE SHOCK

The customs officers were terrifying, even sans Kalashnikovs. They spoke to us confidently, in neither Persian nor Arabic. The only member of my family who met them coolly was my dad, who was still in his turban and clerical garb. I'd watched on the flight as he filled out the arrival card in English. He'd attacked the form with gusto—not simply checking the boxes, but embellishing the questions with additional info.

■ Incoming passenger card ■ Australia
PLEASE COMPLETE IN ENGLISH

▶ Family name: MOHAMMAD   ▶ Given names: JAAFAR

▶ Passport number: IRQ 62190606   ▶ Flight number: Al-Emirates 8109519

▶ Intended Address in Australia:
   In God's hands, Allah-willing near a big mosque in Fawkner Victoria

▶ Do you intend to live in Australia for the next 12 months?   Inshallah

▶ Do you have any criminal convictions?   Yes, many times.

YOU MUST ANSWER EVERY QUESTION—IF UNSURE, YES ☒

▶ Are you bringing into Australia:

1. Goods that may be prohibited, restricted, such as medicines, steroids, illegal pornography, firearms, or illicit drugs?   *(Heaven forbid)*   YES ☐ NO ☒

2. Soil, items with soil attached or used in freshwater areas e.g. shoes?   YES ☐ NO ☒

3. AUD$10,000 or more in Australian or foreign currency equivalent?   YES ☐ NO ☒

4. Goods purchased overseas with a combined value of $900   YES ☐ NO ☒

5. More than 2250mL of alcohol or 50 cigarettes or 50g of tobacco products?   YES ☐ NO ☒
   (Praise Allah we not drinking the alcohol)

6. Animals, parts of animals, animal products including equipment, pet food, birds, fish, insects, shells or bee products?   *(We bring many animals)*   YES ☒ NO ☐

7. Have you been in contact with farms or farm animals in the past 30 days?   YES ☒ NO ☐
   (Contact many animals, not just 30 days, many days)

■ DECLARATION   10/8/1995   **TURN OVER CARD** ▶

Making a false declaration may have serious consequences and can carry a prison term of a maximum 10 years.

He handed the card to an officer, who studied it closely. As he did, his face changed: the universal expression for 'you're in deep shit, sir'. It was a relief that I could read this. He ushered us into a quiet zone.

'Who's this Allah?' he asked my father. 'Is he your legal sponsor?'

'Yes, He sponsors everything.'

'And is that his Christian name?'

'No, not just Christian. Allah is for all humans.'

'…Uh. Yep, what's his surname?'

'Allah is One. He created everything.'

The officer blinked at my father.

'One sec,' he said.

He left the room and came back with another tall, gunless dude.

'Did you fill this out yourself, sir?' the second officer asked. 'You've written here your next residence is in Allah's hands.'

'Yes,' nodded my father. 'Everything in life is in His hands.'

'What's going on, Abu-Osamah?' Mum interjected, in Arabic.

'Nothing, just official matters,' said Dad. 'Wherever we go, they follow.'

'Sir, I need you to speak in English, please.'

From then on, Dad did so. But it wasn't a language problem; it went far deeper than that. He had written 'inshallah' beside 'Are you planning to stay in Australia for the next twelve months?' because, as he explained now, 'It's in God's hands if we stay or not.'

This was very difficult for the customs officers to handle. They explained to my father that we could not enter the country if they were not able to tick a simple 'yes'.

Dad was very firm on this. 'No,' he insisted.

Now, they blinked in unison. 'Okay, hang tight,' they said.

They sent back a man in a suit.

'Morning, sir,' he said cheerfully. 'Mr Mohammad, is it?'

'Almost,' Dad responded.

'Dad, what is he saying?' I asked.

'They're asking my name, just stay put,' he said.

'Your name on the passport is Mohammad,' asserted the suit.

'Abu-Osamah, don't we have visas?' Mum asked.

'Okay, folks, just one at a time,' the man in the suit said. He had a lot more natural composure than the others; I did not know if this was better or worse for us. 'Sir, you have a permanent visa, but my colleagues believe you're saying you won't be staying in the country, is that correct?'

'No,' said Dad, 'I just tell him how can anyone be sure of tomorrow? Except maybe your breakfast, are you sure of your tomorrow?'

The suit peered at Dad. 'If I were to say yes, what would you tell me?'

'I say impossible. No one sure. Only Allah.'

'Right. Yeah, of course.'

'So inshallah we live here. Inshallah a big yes.'

'Let's just amend that to a yes, then, so you can be on your way…'

'No,' said my father. 'Let me tell you a quick story.'

I didn't understand the English, but I knew 'inshallah' well enough to know the story would probably not be quick. Inshallah is one of those weird words that wasn't really built for a brief, efficient definition at a customs desk. For starters, it's not even a word: it's just used like one, but it literally means 'if God wills it'. It's also spoken like a heartbeat for many Muslims, who might use it for 'yes'—after all, nothing is certain:

'Tonight, at my place?'

'Inshallah.'

Meaning, yes, of course, barring an earthquake.

But it's also capable of taking on a more complex shade of meaning, because you might use it to convey exactly the opposite thing. 'Inshallah, I will be at your place tonight' might mean that most certainly you *won't* be there—because if it's in God's hands, you've conveniently left open every possible reason not to go. You are clearly not going, and you are ready to blame God. It's very handy, in every situation other than right now.

'A man walked down the cobbled streets, his lips chapped by the sun,' began my dad, who had never met a parable he didn't like, and on he went for several minutes.

'…Nothing is sure in this life…Always say inshallah, but not after the fact! Before! Okay?' Dad concluded, looking hopefully at the suit.

The suit, of course, just blinked.

'Right,' he said.

'I told him the inshallah story,' Dad informed us cheerfully.

'Wow, go Dad! Converting them to Islam!'

'I was in Iraq, thinking I live in Iraq forever. Then what happened? Saddam happened. I escape to Iran. Thinking I will live *there* forever. Then what happened? Persecution happened. Then I come here…Nothing certain,' Dad concluded.

'So back to this card,' the suit said. 'Basically, there are some answers here which have serious implications for your visa status. What we can do is strip you of your visas and have you deported.'

Cue stunned expression from my dad.

They were specifically concerned about his 'many convictions'. They're the kinds of things that stack up when you're growing up in a country like Iraq, under the rule of a dictator; it didn't help that Dad nodded furiously, and said, 'Yes, jailed many times,' and added that he'd once escaped from prison too.

'What crimes have you been convicted of?'

'Spreading papers against Saddam.'

'Excuse me?'

'I once write on a paper *Down to Dictator* and they jail me, sentence me to die.'

The suit took a relaxed breath. 'Okay, moving on,' he said. 'You've declared you've brought in animals?'

'Yes, in the bags.'

The suit was mystified: they'd already been through all our bags.

Dad was exasperated. 'There!' he said. He gesticulated wildly towards the several cans of sardines, tuna and salmon. Then he looked more cautious. 'Fish in English is also animal, yes?'

Death to nobody!

Imagine there was a war in Australia and you had to flee to Iran. Any Bob or Jane from Perth or Wodonga could just run for their lives and start all over again, no worries, right? All they'd have to do is learn Farsi, the politics, the history and culture. Bob would be, as the saying goes, their uncle.

We had moved to a neighbourhood in the northern suburbs of Melbourne, just metres from the mosque, in exchange for Dad's services as the new imam. Mum returned to her housewife life, but with a fair dinkum difference: she got hooked on the Australian Open and Aussie Rules, and sat glued to the TV for countless happy hours, watching the Bombers take on Carlton and Collingwood. Football, or 'footy', was played with a ball shaped like a watermelon, only it was wearing shoelaces. These factors meant it had a weird bounce; it was not logical like soccer. Mum was fascinated by this, leaving my sisters to do the chores—and leaving me with a lot of time to roam the neighbourhood.

I won't pretend I didn't have my own steep learning curve.

I was excited to buy bread, after the reports Dad had sent home to Iran. He was right; I didn't have to line up at 5 am in the bread queue. But the fact I could buy bread from the petrol station—this I couldn't handle. It was absurd.

The petrol stations—like any public place—were fairylands of absurdity. When you rocked up to this petrol station, at any hour, to buy your bread, nobody was talking about how Australia had come to be. History was taught in school, but wasn't a discussion topic. Instead, everybody was obsessed by the weather. I quickly catalogued the phrases you'd hear people toss around, on the same day, about the same temperature:

'Oh, it's a beautiful day!'
'Oh, it's a great day!'
'Oh, it's a sunny day!'
'Oh, it's a jolly day!'
'Oh, it's a pleasant day!'
'Oh, it's a cracker of a day!'
'Oh, it's a smashing day!'
'Oh, it's a ripper of a day!'
'Oh, will you look at the sun?'
'Oh, will you look at the sunshine?'
'Oh, will you look at the sky?'
'Oh, will you look at *that*?'
'Oh, she's a beauty today.'
'Oh, how about that?'
'Oh, how about that sun?'
'Jeez, it's a warm one!'
'Jeez, it's a beauty out there!'
(In fact, substitute 'jeez' for 'oh' in any of the above.)

One day, Mum asked me to go to the halal butcher to buy some sheep tongue. No problems; I looked up 'tongue' in the dictionary. The Arabic translation for 'tongue' was 'language'; I cross-checked with the Persian dictionary, which confirmed this.

I entered the butcher confidently.

'Good afternoon, sir, can you please give me three languages?'

The butcher looked at me. 'I can only speak two. English and Turkish.'

'No, not *your* languages,' I said. 'I want sheep's languages.' I started desperately pointing at my tongue. 'I want a language like this,' I said. 'The one I am talking with. This language, not your language. Sheep's language.'

This alarmed the butcher, who picked up a large knife and waved me out of the shop.

When I ran out to the street, nobody was chanting 'Death to America'. Or 'Death to Israel'. Or Nepal. Or Senegal. Or Honduras. Death to nobody! Furious chanting, in that moment, might have been comforting.

Police did not take bribes here, which deeply troubled me. I would see them on the street and think, *What if I get into some kind of serious trouble? How do I get out of it?* But this fear was balanced by the fact they seemed not to stomp on people's faces. In fact, nobody stomped on anyone, not teachers, not parents. And yet society stayed disciplined regardless.

Off the streets, it was worse. When you went to people's houses, you did not have to remove your shoes before passing through the door. And yet the houses stayed clean. This was spooky.

And this was just the beginning of your problems. As with the weather—and pork, which was confronting—Australians gave their bathrooms many names. There were *bathrooms* (upper-class usage only), *boys'/girls' rooms* (rare-to-medium usage), *cans* (when a carpenter asked where he'd find one of these, I brought him some tuna in a can), *crappers* (used like cans but more often, especially by builders), *dunnies* (an Australian classic), *honey buckets* (according to the dictionary, though I had never heard it), *johns* (yes! They used the name of their prophet for their faecal chairs), *lavatories* (no one said this, but it was written on the doors), *loos* (like dunnies but more British—why, then, did they use this?), *pissers* (semi-popular with the dunny/crapper crowd), *restrooms* (see *lavatories*), *powder rooms* (used by girls), *shithouses* or *shitters* (both employed by ockers), *urinals* (rare and formal— also strange. Men pissed standing next to each other? They had no shame), *washrooms* (rare, unpopular and boring), and *water closets* (like the WC signs in uncensored Hollywood films. I had always wondered what these letters meant).

People actually sat on toilet seats as if they were dining chairs. But while squats were good for the quads and hamstrings, I had to admit the Western model was overall more ergonomic.

Or it would've been. Many of these toilets, including ours, were allowed to face Mecca. People emptied their bowels in sin all over the country, while facing the house of God. We had to get a plumber in to redirect our own toilet, once we'd all got sick of sitting on it sideways. It was awkward and painful; I almost pulled a hamstring. When the plumber came round, he flushed the toilet, checked the tank and said, 'But your toilet is working!' He did the job, incredulous. It cost a lot of money.

I tried to make friends, but this was a complex process. There was no concept of *taarof*, that Persian custom of declining any offer up to three times before accepting it. At the home of a potential friend, his mother offered me a soft drink. I was parched, but of course said no, thinking she'd ask again twice more. She replied nonchalantly, 'Oh, okay then.' I stayed thirsty throughout the whole three-hour visit.

Another time, I offered a potential friend something to eat. He said no, so I thought, *Okay, he needs the second push.* I asked him again. He said no. I thought, *One final push then*. The third time I offered, he got very angry with me.

The wogs had a slogan for the white Australians: 'Youse came in chains, we came in planes.' But even though such evidence of the white Australians' provenance was all around us, they detested the idea of others coming here by boat. The exception was cruise boats, which everyone seemed to love. I felt like I was losing my mind.

I remembered the simplicity of the imam's lectures, about masturbation and other sins. These had bored me back home, but now, nothing had ever seemed as comforting. In desperation (and also embarrassed to ask Dad), I wrote to a scholar back in Iran.

> **Q:** Esteemed, Revered, Reverend Scholar, Sayyed, may God prolong your life,

I wrote.

> May He prosper and shower you with infinite health and keep you as His servant on Earth and away from all Evil and may the Almighty Creator allow us to bask under your wisdom for decades to come.
>
> Your Highness and Holiness, I often by accident find myself at the beach. Please note these beaches are Western, so women and men are mixed. Moreover, the women are naked. How can I walk along the beach, with the intention of smelling the sea breeze—and only smelling the sea breeze—without accidentally falling into sin?

I was desperate for a loophole to allow me to go to the beach.

> **A:** There is no legal way to enjoy the beach outside Iran. You must wash your eyes in case of contact with women, as well

as perform the semen ablution on your body: head first, then the right part of your body underwater, including genitals, then the left part of your body, also including genitals; after this, you may enter your whole body under the shower.

Do not walk on these sinful strips and stay far away from water and sand and may God protect you under his wide, generous shadow.

P.S. You may also return to the country of Islam and enjoy Iranian beaches, which do not have sinful heathens roaming on them. And to God we belong.

Q: Shopping is a major concern for me, here in Australia. It is riddled with sin and I wanted guidance from Your Excellency on how to do my groceries without entrapping myself.

Firstly, in our supermarkets, there is often background music. I know that music is a sin. Are there types of music that are not sinful by any chance?

These supermarkets also sell alcohol (albeit next door, but owned by the same company). In the presence of alcohol, is buying groceries a sin?

The third part of this question is that most of the cashiers are females (no hijab) and I am forced to look at them. Australians are all about eye contact and it's rude to ignore them. Am I allowed to look at these women, given all this?

The fourth part of the question is that when I hand the female cashier the money, my hand will often (accidentally) touch her hand, skin to skin. How best do I avoid this sin, in your esteemed eyes?

A: You must take extra care shopping in non–God fearing countries.

Music is a sin if 'listened' to. Ask yourself this: are you a listener, or listenee? If you ALLOW music to enter your ear willingly, you are a LISTENER and this is a sin. If music enters your ear unwillingly, you are a LISTENEE and it is not a sin. There is no legal music, although some songs about mothers and war veterans are okay provided they do not tempt you to wiggle your body in sinful ways.

Also, you must shop elsewhere, where alcohol is not sold. If it is the ONLY place where you can shop, you must say God's name and stay as far away from the shop selling sin as possible. We sympathise with your plight.

Also, eye contact with any female is a sin. It leads to fornication, which is a GRAND SIN. Avert your eyes and ignore their customs. Do you want to please them or God? As with music, apply the rule of 'viewer or viewee'. If her face 'falls' in your eye, as in, she happens to be in your field of view, then you are a viewee and it is not a sin. If you allow her to fall in your eyes, and become a viewer, then it is a sin and may God protect us from sin and evil.

Finally, skin contact is deadlier than eye contact and a step closer to fornication. Simply lay the money on the counter. Perform semen ablution in case of accidental contact.

However, I will say this again: it is best you leave the country of impurity and return to Iran, where God's wide shadow protects us from all evil. You will also enjoy all the beaches you desire.

God be with you.

Becoming a Bomber

The country of Australia went by a completely different calendar, one that obviated the New Year and every other celebration we'd organised our lives around in Iran. I'd brought an Iranian diary and used it to keep track of the dates, but it was useless; nobody cared. Even the Australian weekend was discombobulating.

It started on Saturday, which was meant to be the beginning of the week.

What people did care about was the first day of summer. Even the sun seemed to understand this most sacred of dates. It shone differently, extending its flares like a thousand little fingers to caress me. Mum had torn herself away from the TV for the morning and got our first Australian barbecue cranking in the backyard. Moe Greene went to the video store to rent *Crocodile Dundee*.

I rubbed a thick layer of zinc on my face and went out to check the mail. I got there just as the mailman did, perfect timing.

'Hasit guwin, cobber?' he said.

'Excuse me?'

He was about to make a hasty scoot, but he paused to repeat. 'How is it going?' he said slowly.

'Oh, how I am going?' I said. 'Well, today I am not going, because I have a Centrelink appointment with my mum. But yes, usually I am going to language school, Monday to Friday. I am going by bus. I buy zone-two ticket and go to school—'

But I was speaking to the air. After staring at me in utter stupefaction for a moment, the postie had just shaken his head and scooted up the street.

I collected the envelope, and spotted a brochure underneath. At first, I assumed it was just another Pizza Madness Special from Joe's, since his leaflets were red and black like this one. But instead of pizza, this one showed a fighter jet dropping bombs over a large caption: JOIN THE BOMBERS, it said.

I freaked my feathers out and rushed back in to consult with Moe Greene.

'Have you shown this to Dad?' Moe whispered. 'I think it's a test. The Australians want to see if we really want to join or not. Then they can catch Dad.'

We were certain they had secret services everywhere, that every postman and neighbour was a potential spy.

The pamphlet had a number, but I was too afraid to call. They also had a price list, which made me want to get in touch: would they pay us actual money for joining? Suddenly, the Australian summer didn't feel so welcoming; I felt the sun starting to slap me hard across my face and neck. If ever there was a time to use the first swear word I'd learned, it was now. 'Fuck, fuck, fuck,' I said out loud.

Later in the afternoon, we sat around our 'dining table'—actually, in a circle on the floor, the newspapers our ersatz tablecloth. The barbecue was delicious, but it wasn't enough to distract me from the pamphlet. My face was red and flustered, a quality which did not escape the notice of my dad, man of a thousand senses.

'What's with your face?'

'First Aussie sunburn,' I mumbled.

'But you slapped a kilo of that white stuff on your face,' he laughed. 'I know, because you finished the whole tube. If you don't tell me what the story is, I'm afraid you'll miss out tonight.' Dad was in the middle of reading us *1001 Nights*, a nightly practice which I loved.

I looked over at Moe, whose face was poker-magnificent. Had he told our father? No, he wouldn't do that.

I guiltily withdrew the pamphlet from its hiding spot—my socks.

'They think you're a terrorist, Dad.'

To my dismay, he started to laugh.

'Yes, I think we should join and become Bombers, indeed!'

'DAD, NOT SO LOUD—'

Dad raised his hand to shut us up.

'Since we're in Victoria, we must choose a team. And why not the Bombers? We're Muslims, so naturally.' He kept laughing to himself, while we watched him, mouth agape. 'Okay, never, ever repeat that. I'm a cleric, so bad enough. But I say we all start barracking for the Bombers. The other names are boring. The Kangaroos, the Bears, the Lions, the Magpies, the Hawks and Ducks and Geese. God forbid, the Demons!'

He placed the turban on his head, ready for the mosque, where he conducted the nightly prayers. 'Anyway, you lot decide. People are waiting for me.' And he left the house, cool as a cleric with footy fever.

Keeping up with the Joneses

Dad's duties included acting as a marriage celebrant, and that summer he did so for the ecstatic Mr Karimi, whose new wife, an Australian, was now the very weird Mrs Karimi Jones.

They'd invited us to their *Pagosha* ('paa-goshayee'), a party thrown shortly after the wedding, in honour of the newlyweds. The term literally meant 'the spreading of the legs', though the sense behind the phrase lay more in the couple's stepping towards a new venture. The idea was to celebrate their newfound status, as a family.

Mr Karimi was Iranian, but his new family was Aussie—meaning there would be alcohol on offer. Dad felt it would be inappropriate for a cleric to attend, but he asked me, Mum and Moe Greene to go and extend our respects.

The party was unlike anything I had ever seen: *suggestive* music, *suggestive* dancing and, of course, the drinks—no Mr X required.

'My mother-in-law is a bank manager,' boasted Mr Karimi, 'and has helped approve a small business loan for me. I am going to set up a small Persian kebab shop in a city corner.'

His mother-in-law was an elegant woman in her fifties. When she greeted Mr Karimi, he made a point of hugging her and kissing her on the cheeks, calling her 'my second mother'. She passed him a bottle of wine, and he grabbed it gratefully. Then he burst into his thank-you speech.

'Mrs Jones,' he said, effusively. 'Thank you for coming to spread your legs open for me. I hope tonight is not the only time we do this. I hope we're able to do this for many years to come!'

I knew enough English by this time that the wine became the most interesting thing in the room for me—and it was very difficult to keep from laughing.

SLEEPING ROUGH

Mashhad, Iran, 2013: three days until visa expires

The bus pulls into the Mashhad terminal at 2 pm. I can't move my limbs; I've been on that bus for over fourteen hours, in the weird, fitful non-sleep you get on long-haul rides. The driver touches my arm as I descend the steps.

'See? We arrived, without a glitch. And here you were, with all your worries.'

I gape at him, but I guess he has a point: the Kurds, Cleric Job, the soldiers, they all managed to help me, some by active intervention, some by leaving me alone.

The driver, too, in his own way. He winks at me now. 'You hid your headache tablets in that backpack? Spare me.'

I put a finger to my lips and wink back. It's time to find some internet and get back in touch with home.

There's a hot spot here at the terminal; I fire off an email to Ali. I use underlining and all caps: <u>YOU NEED TO CHASE THE FUNERAL DIRECTOR ASAP</u> and *The embassy needs the director's* <u>NAME, ADDRESS AND TELEPHONE NUMBER</u> *to issue the* QUARANTINE PASS. I pray that he understands the urgency.

And then, just in case I'm coming on too strong: *But there is* ABSOLUTELY *no need to panic. All is under control.*

I hop in a cab and head straight to the Department of Foreign Affairs. It's dog-eat-dog here, people scrambling. I shove my way to the appropriate window.

I'm face to face with a female soldier, in full black hijab. Thick glasses. I notice her rank stitched on her chador and address her accordingly; I then hand her the dossier, and get her up to speed.

'Your father was an Afghan?' she asks, nonchalantly.

'His passport is Australian.'

'Are you being smart with me?'

'No, ma'am. He's Australian.'

'Of what origin?'

'Why does that matter? He is an Australian citizen, full stop.'

She looks at me squarely. 'Do you want to take his body back? If so, you answer my questions.'

'Ma'am, please. Can you just go by my documents, not the colour of my skin?'

'Oof. Nelson Mandela, are you?'

'What do you want to hear? Okay, yes, I am an Arab.'

'Then you will need to go to building H on the East Wing and fill out a pink form.'

'But I am Australian.'

'That's what your paper says. Your origin will always be Iraq. You are not special, so don't parade here telling us what to do. Do as I tell you and you won't have any problems.'

Dejected, I pull out from the window. Two people fight to replace me. I look at the time—3.40 pm. It's almost closing time again. But there's nothing to do but follow the signs until I reach a booth marked *Aliens*.

'Sir, I would like a pink form please,' I say.
'They're only for foreigners,' the soldier replies.
'That I am.'
'Pretty fluent for an Arab.'
'Do I take this pink form back to the main hall?'
'Yes, and it costs five thousand.'

I pay the fee and fill out the form. Most questions clearly don't apply to me; it's only relevant to Iraqis without an identity. But I do my best, and use my football training to hip-and-shoulder-bump my way back through the crowd to the female soldier. I place the pink form in front of her.

The lady studies it.

'This isn't filled,' she concludes, unmoved.

'Some questions don't apply to me. Like that one that says why have you left Iraq. I was born here.'

She continues studying the form, then picks up a red pen. She draws a long, thick line across the form to render it void and throws it in the bin.

I want to gape at her, but she won't meet my eyes. Instead, she finds a new paper, stamps it twice and signs it. She then stamps it again, seals it in an envelope and stamps it one more time. Each thud of the stamp makes my eye twitch. I focus on my breathing.

'Go to the Department of Births and Deaths and register your father as deceased,' she says. 'They will issue a death certificate. You bring that back here.'

'And that's it?' I say.

'Have you booked your tickets?'

'I can't, without an exit paper.'

'Then you'd better get a move on. Friday and Saturday are public holidays, you know.'

Believe me, I know. 'Thank you,' I tell her. I leave the rest unsaid.

❖ ❖ ❖

I cab it back to the airport to pick up my luggage. The manager with the unfashionable hat is drinking tea again.

'You are back.' He smiles.

'Thank you for looking after my luggage,' I say, and mean it.

'The least I can do for a guest of my country.'

I reach for my pocket, but he grabs my hand, like my father did, before I can withdraw the gratuity notes.

'Don't you dare. You are a guest,' he says.

At first, I think he's just doing *taarof*, so I offer him cash again. I offer again and again. But the man is deadly serious.

'Your father has passed away in a sacred land,' he says, 'and you are clearly fatigued. Keeping your luggage here isn't worth a thank you. It was my duty. I hope someday if I am in your country and in need, then you will be there for me. If not for me, then someone else. Go, and God be with you.'

I lug the bags away, stunned.

❖ ❖ ❖

The cheap hotels are all booked out, I know that from the other night, so I walk into a five-star option, about $400 a night. I have no idea how I will afford the room, but the temperature is still on zero, so I really have no choice.

The concierge barely looks at me. 'We are full,' he blurts out.

I stare him down and march up to reception.

'And this hotel might not be the right choice for you,' he calls after me.

I address the clerks in English, which makes them look up. But the concierge wasn't lying. They're as full as anywhere.

I swallow my pride and ask if I can rest four or five hours in the lobby, taking out $100 worth and begging with my eyes.

The receptionists don't answer me; instead, they look behind me. I follow their eyes. The lavish lobby wants nothing more than to chew me up and spit me out. Well-dressed people bustling, even at midnight: kings and queens stay here. I get the message and haul my father's bags into the night.

❖❖❖

I stagger through a dark alley, running on my last fumes. I stumble across a woman and three children spread across a hessian sack. She cradles two of the children on her lap like kittens; the other rests against her shoulder. My knees go weak. The five-star hotel is just metres from here.

I place my luggage, guitar and Dad's cane to one side and sit beside the woman, not quite on the hessian sack, but not too far away either.

'Aren't you cold?' I ask.

'No, son, are you?' The woman shivers.

I don't know what to say to her. I just gaze at the ground.

'Are you here for the pilgrimage?' she asks. Her voice is hoarse, but loving.

'I was,' I say. 'But my father passed away first, so I'm taking him back home.'

'I'm sorry to hear that,' she says. 'I'm sure God will not only find him a place in paradise, but host him well.'

I keep my eyes cast down, still unsure what to do. 'Mother, why are you here?' I ask.

'Do you really want to hear it, son?' she says. 'Don't you have somewhere to be?'

'Even if I did, I want to hear it. But no pressure, please, I'm just a curious boy.'

'No,' she says, 'I can tell you are a good boy, too. The reason

I am here is that my husband was a drug addict. He was also a hard worker. But he saw bad things in the war. Sometimes people just fall apart through no fault of their own. Eventually, the police took him. His boss was a good man too. He gave me some money but it ran out fast. His relatives didn't want to help. They said I enabled him. And my own family—well.'

I don't have to ask: the war.

She nods at the child on her shoulder. 'This one is my sister's. The other two are mine. I came and sat here last week, thinking the rich people might help. They didn't. But I can't walk anywhere else anymore. No energy.' She shrugged. 'So I stayed here.'

'When does your husband come back?' I ask.

'Never,' she replies simply. 'A creditor ordered a hit on him. He was killed in jail.'

At the mouth of the alley, the five-star hotel is still bustling. Behind it shines the golden dome of the holy shrine.

'Do you mind if I rest here tonight?'

'You'll get sick from the cold,' she replies.

'Maybe,' I say. 'But I think I was meant to meet you.'

She closes her eyes. 'I'm not special, son. There are thousands just like me. But God is great.'

I sleep for a few hours. I check my watch: 5.30 am. It's still dark and freezing; daylight feels very far from here.

I'm using Dad's garb to keep warm, but the winter has no mercy. I get up quietly, trying not to wake the woman or the children. The woman wakes.

'Be safe, son,' she says.

I dig into my pocket and drop the contents on the ground. I don't look at it, but I decide that whatever comes out is hers; whatever it is, I know it's at least a month's worth of food.

She doesn't look at it either, but she knows too. 'That's too much, son,' she says.

She starts crying. I don't want to make a big deal of it, and I don't know what to do. So I let her kiss me on the cheek, then grab my things and leave.

LESSONS TO LEARN

Melbourne, Australia, 1995–97

Nailed it

In school, I was placed in a class with other kids like me: losers who couldn't speak the language. English was taught by Ms Hunter, a woman in her early forties who had a way of making sure every student listened to her with absorbed rapture. It had to do with her choices of clothing, which made her look a decade younger, a decade feistier and a decade spicier.

Ninos was the dirtiest and naughtiest of us all—a horny, acne-prone nineteen-year-old Christian Iraqi. He had failed this class twice before, which he insisted was nowhere near a deliberate attempt to clock more hours in the presence of Ms Hunter's 'saucy wagon'.

That saucy wagon had some interesting ideas. Ms Hunter was a three-time divorcee, and liked to engage us in debates over why Arab men were permitted to marry four wives, while their wives were distinctly not afforded that luxury.

Enter yours painfully.

Upon my arrival in Ms Hunter's class, I quickly established myself as the resident philosopher with worse English than anybody's, who nonetheless liked to challenge everyone on everything. I was already in her bad books for saying 'sex-cuse me' ('It's *excuse me*'), and for accidentally calling her old (when she was forced to explain the finer points of 'Miss', which was used for younger single women, versus 'Mzzz', which was for women like herself).

'*Sex*-cuse me, *Mzzzz* Hunter,' I said. 'Let me telling you why Muslim man can marry four womans and one woman cannot marry four mans.' It was a regular sermon. 'Okay, you have a container of water, in it one litre of water and you pour the water in four glasses. Good?'

She gave a brief nod.

'Very good. So we have four water coming from one source. If I ask you, Mzzz Hunter, the first glass of water, who it comes from, you will say the container. I say the second glass, who it come from? You say still container. But! If I take glasses and pour them back in container, can you tell me which water belong to which glass? Of course no! All is mixed. You do not know which is which.'

'So what?' she said, sceptically.

'So. When there is one container, ONE MAN'—it was time to bring home the analogy—'his children all have one father. But if woman marry four husbands, and she has children, *who is father*? You don't know. All mixed. See, Islam think of everything,' I concluded, pleased as a cock in the morning.

'You can get DNA testing,' she flatly replied.

'What this one, DNA?' I asked.

'It's a scientific test which reveals who the father is.'

'But the container...I was told it is always right,' I exhaled, face reddening.

'I'm not sure you've quite nailed this one, Osamah.'

At the bus stop that afternoon, I consulted with Moe Greene. Even though he didn't go to a language school, he still caught the bus with me.

Moe Greene was a street-smart boy, with a heart soft enough to feed the entire planet twice over yet hard enough to withstand its worst volcanoes: strong, short-tempered, no-fuss Moe. He'd named himself Moe Greene after watching *The Godfather*. In the film, Fredo tells Michael Corleone not to speak aggressively at a character named Moe Greene: 'Don't you know who that is? That's *Moe Greene*!'

'Moe!' I said. 'You know my teacher, the one who always makes me sin.'

'Why?'

'One day red dress, one day pink dress, one day pink and red dress, one day dress so low I see a vertical line where her chest is…but anyway, she is divorced three times.'

'Nothing wrong with strong car with a little mileage,' shrugged Moe. Even at eleven, he was a bit ahead of me sexually.

'Why is Ms Hunter like a car? Anyway, she said something weird in class today—she said I didn't nail something, like with a hammer. Any ideas on that one?'

'Of course!' he enthused. 'Come with me!'

We alighted the bus at the hardware store.

The next day, I snuck into the classroom early. It was already decorated with the results of our assignments, all our artwork clipped and pinned to the walls—lots of refugee slogans about peace and equality. I was determined to up the ante.

I whipped out my brand-new hammer and proceeded to nail a framed essay on the wall outlining my views on the issue of Arab men and plural marriage. Moe Green's words from the hardware store echoed through my mind:

'They celebrate your point of view here in Australia, even if it's fucked.'

I'd even spell-checked the essay. It looked damn good on the wall; there was no way I hadn't nailed it.

I sat there smiling at my desk as everyone filed into the room, led by Ms Hunter, this time in a pink dress. I couldn't wait for my reward.

Learning a big lesson in a one-week window

A lot of time in the classroom was devoted to analogy, as in 'pig is to pork as cow is to beef'.

'Mzzz! Mzzz!' I buzzed.

'Yes, Osamah,' Ms Hunter said.

'I cannot retain that example in my head.' Pork, of course, was illegal in Islam.

'Right, just settle down, we'll try again. Pen is to author as brush is to artist; lyrics are to a lyricist as music is to a composer.'

'Mzzz, we don't listen to music either. It's a sin,' I said.

Ninos jumped in. 'Don't listen to him, Ms Hunter. This boy comes from a radical city, radical upbringing, radical everything.'

'Hmm,' Ms Hunter hummed. 'Alright. I'll give you a sentence; you fill in the blanks.'

'Which you, Mzzz?' I asked.

'All of you.'

'Ms Hunter,' I said. 'English is funny. You is you as in just-you, as in everybody-you. Very misleading.'

Ms Hunter was used to dealing with interruptions like these. She acknowledged them and quickly moved on. 'Here's the sentence. Ice is to Eskimos as desert is to…?'

'Arabs,' Lara replied.

Lara was a seventeen-year-old Christian Iraqi who I always managed to sit directly behind. Her hair was wild and wavy.

Ninos liked to tease her for being overweight, which she was, but still I saw a rainbow every time she spoke.

'Well done! Very good, Lara!' Ms Hunter applauded.

'Some Arabic countries don't have desert, but,' I said.

'It's a generalisation, but it works in this instance, so it's fine,' she said cheerily.

'Ms Hunter, I have analogy for Osamah,' Ninos quipped. 'He is annoying like fingernails on the blackboard.'

'Very good, Ninos,' she said. 'Very, very good. But, you know—be gentle, next time. I'll give you all a one-week window to come up with a good analogy, and then we'll come back and share them in class.'

'One-week window, Mzzz?' I asked.

It was one too many questions. 'Yes, and I need coffee.' She got up and left in the middle of class.

At the bus stop, I consulted Moe Greene again: the human dictionary.

'One-week window,' I offered.

'Bro. Very easy indeed. I know a guy,' he said. 'Come with me.'

We ended up, of course, at a glass shop off Sydney Road.

'We need a one-week window,' I said, a bit too serious. 'Do you have in stock?'

'Not sure what you mean, mate,' said the scrawny sales guy. 'You mean make it in one week?'

'Yes, yes,' I said impatiently. 'What's the best you can do?'

'What sort of size were you looking for?'

I considered this. 'It's for a classroom.'

'Rightio, well, we've got plenty of options, but if you wanted something simple…'

'No, not simple,' I replied. 'I want something very, very outstanding.'

This was going to be difficult for the best budget I could offer, but the salesman had some glass he said he didn't need. 'You don't even have to wait a week,' he said happily. 'You can pick it up right now.'

So I rocked up to class at eight-fifteen the following morning, having lugged a window-sized width of glass there on the bus. I strode straight to Ms Hunter's desk and leaned the glass against the wood. She'd given us a week; I'd got it done in twenty-four hours.

Needless to say, I was her favourite student.

Guessing Ms Hunter's age

On Ms Hunter's birthday, she sat behind her desk sipping coffee from one of her many Parisian-themed mugs. This one read, *J'adore Paris*.

It was adorned with a picture of a gorgeous French *siren*, a phrase that I'd picked up when many others eluded me. I used it everywhere; I couldn't help myself. This beautiful continent was swathed in sirens.

Ms Hunter not the least of them. She wore a bright orange dress today, and lubricated the edge of her mug with her splendid lips. I watched closely as the residue of her rich red lipstick ringed the fancy mug with additional glamour.

She wouldn't say how old she was today. When I'd pressed her, she told me it was rude to ask a woman her age. So I'd gone ahead and bought a card and guesstimated forty-four.

It seemed like a safe number. If I tried forty, she might say, 'What, you think I'm still a kid?' If I guessed fifty, she might well tell me off for thinking she was old.

To my surprise, the other kids' desks were totally free of birthday presents. I didn't want anyone to think I was sucking up. But the respect I paid my teachers was the same as that I paid my parents—teachers *taught* me. Without people like

LESSONS TO LEARN

Ms Hunter, I just had Moe and Ninos. Moe was responsible for the hardware-store and window-shopping disasters. All Ninos had taught me was how to blow up condoms like balloons.

True to this logic, I approached the desk.

'Happy birthday, Mzzz,' I said, proudly brandishing the card and a gift-wrapped box which contained a Persian cuisine cookbook. My mother had selected this on a trip to Kmart, the theory being that Australians needed to learn to cook proper food.

'Why, thank you, Osamah,' Ms Hunter replied, stuttering from the shock. 'That is very kind. I'm not sure if I can accept it.' She began to get very emotional.

'Mzzz. Can I sing "Happy Birthday" in Persian to you, and then English, because I have never done it in both languages?'

She looked at me, eyes welling up. I burst out in Persian, chanting '*Tavalodet Mobarak, Tavalodet Mobarak…*'

Lara jumped in, asking if she could do it in Arabic. So together, we chanted: '*Sana helwa ya gameela, Sana helwa Anesa Hunter…*'

Now other Arabic speakers joined us, joyous. It gave me goosebumps. The classroom roared with 'Happy Birthdays'. A couple of Chinese students piped up in their native language; others followed: Indian, Vietnamese and Urdu.

It was too much for Ms Hunter. I wished I could freeze the moment. She never told us how old she was; if she was offended by the estimate I'd written on the card, she never showed it. I was probably wrong, but I didn't care, and still don't. I had got it right, invoking our mighty chorus of 'Happy Birthdays'—the details themselves were unimportant.

Nude soldiers

As I was packing up to go home, two hands slapped over my eyes, rendering me sightless.

'Guess who?' Ninos whispered hoarsely. He was so lazy, he didn't bother to disguise his voice.

He let go. 'Hey, I left something in class,' he said. He opened his desk drawer and whisked out a magazine. 'Wanna see?'

'Yes, I love magazines,' I said seriously. 'What's the topic?'

He turned around, exaggerating the conspiracy. I rolled my eyes, then wandered over and looked at the magazine.

OH.

MY.

GOD.

It was a picture of a woman.

Her legs were open at 180 degrees.

She was holding a machine gun.

The questions demolished me. What side did she fight for? Where the hell was her combat gear? Why did her face look sleepy, but, you know, different sleepy? And did all girls' genitalia look like that?

But I pulled back. 'No, Ninos! I don't want to look at that!'

He shrugged and closed the magazine.

'No,' I moaned. 'Just one more peek.'

He grinned, and spread the centrefold again.

'No!' I yelped. 'That's horrible. Show me another page.'

He gladly flipped to a fresh picture, this one of a woman wearing a stethoscope and nurse's cap. Her legs were spread like a Thanksgiving turkey.

'No more,' I pleaded.

He giggled and tucked the magazine into his bag. But the magazine had shocked a moment of honesty out of me. 'Ninos,' I said, heart thudding. 'I want to ask Lara the question. I want to ask her if she'd like to eat a sandwich with me in the yard.'

'You dog,' he howled. 'Go watch some sexy movies and learn some proper English! Girls don't want your sandwiches.

They want you to pound them. In the movies I watch, they scream so.'

'No, no, no,' I said vehemently. 'Lara is a good girl.' The truth was, I wouldn't have minded getting naughtier with Lara—the sandwich was designed as a test. If she said yes to the sandwich and things were going well, I thought maybe we could share a smoothie too.

Ninos squinted at me like I was a mental patient, and he was a doctor about to declare me a lost cause. He left the classroom without adding a word, the magazine of dark treasures going with him.

The proposal

The end-of-school bell had already gone. I had built up the courage to show Lara my poem. I made it sound fancy using a few solid English words I had learned. The most exciting part was that yesterday I had learned the word *brine*—not in class but rather after buying canned fish in a supermarket aisle—and I made a quick edit so the poem could sound even fancier.

> **A poem by Osamah Sami Al-Bakiry, 22/11/1995**
> In the name of God, the Beneficent, the Merciful
> Thanks to the Lord for being beautiful
> And giving me brains and pens to write
> For Lara
>
> When I gaze out of window
> The day is hazy
> I don't want to do anything today
> I am not lazy
> I am just crazy (by you)
>
> You are the tuna and I am the brine
> The can is our house, our shrine

I grinned over at Lara. It was hard to gauge whether she loved my work or absolutely loved it. Just as she went to pass the paper back to me, Ninos pinched it from her hand and began to read it out loud. 'Being Picasso with the ladies, huh?'

'Picasso was painter, idiot.' I hit back, but seeing Ninos's nose widen like a dragon, I immediately regretted my words. 'You know what, Ninos…' I whimpered, as I braced for an incoming punch. 'I think Picasso occasionally wrote poetry.'

'I wanted to say to you this is good shit. It is shit still, but good shit.' Ninos handed back the poem. Seeing him half-impressed by my work was impressive in itself.

'Thank you, Ninos. It meaning a lot to me for you to say this. I spent many hours and many dictionary pages to write it.'

'Okay, relax, I didn't say you Einstein. Just Picasso.'

'Ninos, in Iran, they have Persian saying: "real praise come from your enemy". So I thank you a lot.'

'You mention Iran again you better be my enemy.' He replied, agitated. 'My father he fight against Iran in war…But he died.'

'Sorry, Ninos. I had uncle who died in war too.'

'No, no. My father died in a car accident, delivering chickens to Mosul. His truck tip over edge.'

I looked at Ninos. He was pretending not to care about his loss, but there was a whole house of pain visible behind the windows of his soul. Lara and I paused for a brief moment to ponder Ninos's words.

'Okay, everyone…' Lara broke the minute's silence. 'I see you all after the weekend.'

'Lara, wait, you not tell me what you thinked of my poem.'

'Your tuna poem?' she responded.

Lara grabbed my poem, quickly wrote a few digits down and, rushing out, she delivered a blow to my head: 'Give me a ring on the weekend.'

I tried to: a) digest her words and b) tell her goodbye. So I shouted back: 'Drive safely and don't die in a car accident like Ninos's father.'

He punched me flush on the shoulderblade. His knuckles bore the brunt. 'Dude! She told you to give her a ring.'

'Yes. But I am too young for marriage.'

Ninos went to say something but stopped himself. He assembled one of his impish smiles. 'Yeahhhhs. Exactly. She wants you to give her a *wedding* ring.'

'I already know, Ninos. But I am fourteen. And she is not Muslim. And I don't have money for ring.'

'Chill pill! First, she not teasing you. She is sooooo into you. She always looking at you when you not looking. You can not see because you are not looking. It is like when you want to see yourself blink in front of mirror. Impossible. She is like your blink. Always looking when you not looking. Two, yes, you are young but in your culture, men marry young all the times. Thirdly, she is not Muslim but she love you, and that is what is important. Was Juliet Muslim? No. Did Romeo care she that was not Muslim? No. But don't tell anyone about this, they will not believe you,' Ninos carefully deliberated.

'But you are my witness.'

'No. People will think we are fooling them.'

I had been shocked a lot in my life, but this moment tasered me comatose. Had my poem affected Lara this much? Perhaps the poem was the straw that broke the camel's back? It was the final gust that tipped her over towards marriage.

At home, I reached for my charity box, which contained about $40. Donating money as a Muslim is as natural as drinking tap water. It's a part of life, a *source* of life. We are constantly reminded that a donation will wipe away seventy-two inflictions, or ordeals, from the day. Who wouldn't donate knowing there are seventy-two curses awaiting them? It is insurance against evil. My left-shoulder angel was telling me I was *technically* poor in the eye of God and I should break the piggy bank. My right angel was taking a snooze. Just when I needed him.

I relented and grabbed a knife and pierced my charity tin.

On Monday, I was edgy and excited. Before long, Lara arrived, smelling like a meadow.

'Osamah, you were supposed to give me a ring on the weekend!'

'On the weekend?' My eyes twitched like a madman. 'Is it too late now?'

'That's okay, we'll talk at lunchtime.'

But I couldn't take it any longer. Somewhat sweaty, I winked over at Ninos and flashed a small jewellery box to him. Now I saw *his* eyes twitch. I felt he wanted to tell me something but the cat had his tongue. Just as Ms Hunter walked in class, I stood up and asked everyone to be quiet. The chitchat stopped. I turned to Lara smiling, genuinely happy and genuinely nervous. I got on one knee, raising the cubical container, revealing a polished second-hand silver ring, still with the Cash Converters price tag attached.

Gruesome one-upmanship

In class the next week, Ninos was bragging about his dad. 'He was martyred in the war,' he said casually—the highest form of honour in a classroom like ours.

But for all Ninos's strange powers, his memory wasn't great. Just last week, he'd told us his father had perished in his chicken truck, which had tipped into a ravine en route to their farm.

'He took three bullets to the chest,' he insisted now, 'but a month later, there he was, fighting just as hard. When they finally shot him dead, he took down a full platoon.'

The lie was obvious, and so was the cause. Bojan the Serb had kicked off the round of conversation by proclaiming his grandfather's indisputable heroism, and Ninos couldn't risk his own lineage looking comparatively weak. Death by chicken truck was a liability.

But Bojan just one-upped him. 'My grandfather,' he said confidently, 'fought without any of his limbs. And he took down a whole *brigade* before they captured him.'

'They had to shoot my father at point-blank range,' countered Ninos. 'They shot him from afar, to no effect.'

When these kinds of volleys happened, as they often did, Ms Hunter just sat there behind her desk, going pale. She couldn't handle these tales of tremendous slaughter—but we were talking about our forebears, so what could you do? Was she really going to be the one to douse these conversations with cold water? We sounded nonchalant about them, but who knew how we felt? We'd come to her classroom from all kinds of places.

For my part, I was a fourteen-year-old boy, and totally incapable of staying quiet while other kids tried to show each other the size of their balls. I made the heat hotter with the story of my uncle Adnan and his elite tank-defusing regiment. The fact that it involved a schoolteacher—the enemy commander—made Ms Hunter's face all the paler, which meant that I'd won. Or was close to winning, when Lara jumped in.

'The bald woman boasts of her niece's hair,' she proclaimed. 'You three are bald women. Quit it.'

This was enough to embarrass us—and enough to mortify me, being called out on my transparency by Lara. I excused myself from the classroom, feeling flushed and stupid.

I came back in bearing a glass of ice water and offered it to Ms Hunter, who accepted it with understated gratitude. I didn't dare look at Lara, but my heart thumped, somersaulted, pounded.

I may not have impressed her with my borrowed war stories, but maybe I'd won the day by doing something quieter.

Girl on fire

The paradise of Ms Hunter's class was not the kind that could last. I felt increasingly hangdog. Lara hadn't shown up all week.

'Ninos,' I eventually whispered. 'Do you know where Lara is?'

He leaned across to me when Ms Hunter's back was turned. 'Recovering from the pumping I gave her last night.' He winked. 'No, idiot. She was too good for us. They sent her to high school.'

I raised my hand and interrupted the lesson. 'Mzzz Hunter!' I howled. She whipped around. 'Is it true that Lara's in high school?'

'I believe so, Osamah,' she said. 'When someone's on fire like that, you can't keep them in this kind of class!'

My eyes went googly with horror. I wanted to cry, but Ninos seemed to be cool about it.

I excused myself to the toilet. This was my favourite new trick; I couldn't believe that Ms Hunter granted permission, every time. Back home in Iran, you'd have been flogged just for asking.

This time, I rushed straight to the payphone just outside the Language Centre, dialling information and requesting the hospital.

'Which hospital?' asked the operator.

'Any,' I gasped.

They connected me to the Royal Melbourne.

They had no record of Lara.

I frantically dialled two more hospitals. No record of her there, either.

A businesswoman was waiting in line for the payphone, tapping her foot. She did this hard enough for me to hear it behind the glass doors. I glanced over my shoulder. She made a point of exhaling—'*ooooofffff*'—and checking her watch. I was getting nowhere.

'Sex-cuse me, miss,' I said, opening the door. 'I am trying to locate a friend who catched fire in class but she isn't in any hospital. I am worried her beautiful hair is burned.'

The businesswoman stopped tapping her foot. Her hand clapped over her mouth.

'She caught fire in class?' the woman said. 'Oh, you poor little boy.'

'Yes,' I nodded sombrely. 'My teacher said she's on fire so they moved her up to high school.'

The businesswoman went from distraught to angry in a hundredth of a second. 'That's a very bad joke,' she grumbled. 'Shouldn't you be in school?'

She pushed past me. I copped a feel, but never saw the burning girl again.

First date

My grief over Lara was briefly forestalled by the publication of my article. It was just the school newsletter but, for a language student, this was a very big deal. I couldn't believe it was happening, but there it was: splashed across pages three and four, sandwiched between the canteen menu and an ad for netball practice.

> ### My View on Refugees
> I really think refugees are important. Not only for driving taxis but other jobs too. Did you know some refugees are even doctors? My dad is a doctor. He has two doctorates and is a leader and visionary in the community. He has been a refugee twice in his life because of the war and fate. He is just one example of the abundance number of refugees who excel

> beyond stereotype. Does it surprise you to know that there are refugees who do NOT receive social benefits of Centrelink?
>
> Mr John Howard is treating refugees not nicely. But I can guarantee Mr Howard that we are not scary. We eat and go to the toilet just like him. Yes, we do only eat halal meat and no pork, but we still eat other animals and good vegetables. I know Mr Howard loves cricket. I too love cricket. I play cricket. And I'm a refugee. So if it were mathematics, Mr Howard would naturally like me.
>
> Mr Howard, I like how you don't like guns and did the gun buy-back which shows you don't like to see people dead, and many refugees die if they stay in their own countries, so please accept them to this beautiful country. We have so much space.
>
> I invite you, Mr Prime Minister, to enjoy a game of cricket with refugees and see that we all have hearts. God be with you, mate.

Precocious, no? As if I couldn't have been prouder, it somehow caught the attention of a white girl.

> Hi Osamah,

the email read.

> I know you attend Brunswick High but I go to Coburg Girls and they published your article in my school newsletter too! I wish there were more people like you who took these issues seriously, instead of just worrying about what eggs to throw at the teachers' cars on muck-up day.
>
> Nadia

I stared at my screen. A girl had emailed me? I was meant to be concentrating on a polynomial exercise sheet for maths class, but clearly I had bigger fish to fry.

> I chewed it over for a whole two days before writing back.
>
> Hello Nadia,

I carefully began.

> I think it's fascinating that there are students like you who care that there are students like me who care. You sound like a lovely girl.
>
> Yours very sincerely,
> Osamah

That same day, Nadia wrote back to say I sounded like a lovely guy, too! She was lovely; I was lovely; we were both lovely. I was in.

> Good Very Morning Nadia,

I grandly replied.

> I'm sending this before I go to school. I don't know how often you check your emails but I am checking them daily. I have dial-up internet but as long as there are no pictures it loads fast. But if you want to send me a picture, that'd be awesome. I won't stare at it for too long. I wish I went to your high school so I can see you face to face. I bet you are lovely, I can tell, from how you write. I will check my email very shortly from the computer rooms at school (sneaky) and talk again.
>
> Yours most faithfully,
> Osamah

By the following evening, Nadia still hadn't written back. So I opened a new message and carefully started again.

> Hi Nadia,
> I checked my email yesterday and today and you haven't responded. I think you have had enough of my emails? I will write other articles and maybe that way you will talk to me again.
>
> Somehow in these last seven days I have felt some connection although I haven't seen you. I will check my email again to see if you will be replying.
>
> Regards,
> Osamah

An excruciating week went by, refreshing and refreshing my browser. When Nadia finally wrote back, I couldn't believe my eyes.

> Hey Osamah!
> So sorry, my grandmother's relo died. Sad but we ended up going to Port Douglas so a bit of a relaxation too.
>
> Do u wanna meet up?
>
> Nads xx

Sure I did.

> Hey Nads,

I wrote, cool as a cucumber.

> I am so sorry about your grandmother's relo. We say 'to God we belong and to Him we return' and I hope she is in Heaven. I believe we all go to Heaven even if you are not Muslim. Are you Muslim? That would be better.
>
> And I will be very, very happy to meet up. It has to be after school but not too late so I can tell my parents I am going to library.

So, there is a park in Brunswick behind my school and there aren't too many Iraqi taxi drivers there (I can't be seen with a girl where they assemble as it will have consequences). I will wait for you by a bench, which is near the toilet blocks. It will be easy to spot me!

Did I tell you I am an actor and I can do accents? I can do the mafia accent, I will show you when I see you!

Yours with respect,
Osamah

P.S. I asked a friend what xx means (you put at end of your email) and he said to me xx are rude internet websites. I think you may have done that accidentally.

Then I panicked, and opened a fresh email. I added, all in a fluster:

Nadia hello!
Just to let you know the toilet blocks are normally locked so best to go to the bathroom at your school before coming to meet me.

Best unfiltered regards,
Osamah

She agreed to meet on a hot Thursday after school. I sat nervously on the park bench. Some kids had graffitied an industrial-sized penis on the wall.

It was stiflingly hot, and I regretted my outfit choice as the minutes ticked on: a shirt, tie and suit jacket I'd hurriedly donned in the locker room after class.

I chewed a little gum, to enhance my mouth's natural flavours.

I dipped into the tub of hair gel in my bag; my hair was lousy with sweat. While I was still mashing it through the sodden strands, a voice called across the park.

'Osamah!'

I was stunned. *This* was Nadia? She was gorgeous.

I stood up to shake her hand, then retracted the offer.

'Sorry, I have gel on my hands.'

'You're funny.'

'Thanks, it's a curse.'

I sat back down on the bench. She didn't join me.

'What's with the suit?' she asked me. 'Are you going to a wedding or something?'

'Yes,' I nodded, grateful for the easy out. 'I think there's some kind of wedding. Why, don't you like it?'

'Aren't you hot?'

'I think *you're* hot,' I said quickly. 'I mean, hot like the weather can be hot. Yeah, it's a hot day because it's hot.'

Awkward silence followed this, so I took the invitation to fill it.

'How about that sun, huh? They say it's millions of light years away and still it's so hot. No wonder we want to move to Mars. Sit down, please.'

I patted the bench.

'Here?' she asked. A drain had burst in the toilet block, and she sniffed at the stink.

Despite the smell, she sat down gingerly and stared straight ahead.

We sat like that for a few minutes, dead silent, side by side.

At one stage, I loosened my tie.

Finally, Nadia got up.

'Hey, nice to meet you,' she said breezily. 'I just remembered I have to babysit tonight. Gotta go, or my mum will *kill* me!'

I followed Nadia with my numb eyes as she walked away. My hand was still sticky, so I couldn't even shake her hand.

Objectively, this was a total bomb-out, a total choke. But I couldn't help feeling a weird kind of elation.

I'd just had my very first date.

Bikini angles

At school, they taught us that liquid could turn to gas at the right temperatures. But today, the hottest day, the kind of day that could vaporise you, school was far from our minds.

It was finally time for me and Moe Greene to see the famous Australian beach.

We'd once been to the beach in Iran, a casual six-hour drive from Qom; it was cold and cloudy, and the water grey and sad. From this excursion, I'd learned a trip to the beach was a formal occasion, and today I'd donned my best outfit, hoping to make an impression: a snazzy shirt, duly ironed, and black pants.

We tromped off the tram, soaking with sweat.

Suddenly, the sky opened up. Vast blue seas. Bluer than any blue I'd seen, the bluest blue in nature.

First, the beauty—then the shock. Nobody was dressed up like Moe Greene and me. We were Eskimos in the Sahara.

'Seriously, bro,' spat Moe Greene. His jeans were sweaty and drenched. 'Why did you tell me to dress like this—oh, Osamah, holy moly.'

Our breaths arrested as soon as we saw the women. It wasn't just that they weren't dressed up; they were wearing basically nothing. Some of them, literally nothing. Even the women who wore bikinis flashed angles I hadn't known existed. Even my best wet dreams were revealed to be profoundly unimaginative.

'Let's count them,' I said.

'The people? Are you nuts?'

'No, just the ones without tops.'

To do this, we scurried behind a pair of large beachside rocks, for fear of being spotted by the ubiquitous Iraqi taxi drivers. This made us look deeply suspicious, pointing and gawking.

This was the heaven the Koran had promised us, right here in Australia.

I counted fifteen, sixteen, seventeen…

We stayed there for hours, burning up.

PAPERWORK IS PAPERWORK

Mashhad, Iran, 2013: two days until visa expires

It's 6 am, still cold, still dark. Three hours' sleep in an alley. My dad's cane and luggage. My luggage. My guitar.

I haul them to a main road and try to hail a cab. Twenty minutes. No one stops. They all have somewhere to be.

An old, run-down, lightless car trails to a stop by my feet. The driver is an old man, eyes filled with history. He winds down the window with a slow, manual creak. It jams a couple of times, but he forces. It's finally down, but only just.

'Where, my boy?'

'Actually, I'm looking for a taxi. But thanks.'

'I can be your taxi.'

'A taxi will be cheaper, thank you.'

'I'll charge you the same fee.'

'No, but thank you, sir.'

'You know what,' he says, 'you'll get cold out here.' He pops the boot and clambers out. 'I'll take you wherever you want, for free.'

'That's very kind, sir. But you mustn't.'

'Of course I must,' he says. 'I see a person freezing, it's my duty to help.' He smiles at me. I notice his yellowed teeth, and dark gaps where three are missing.

'Listen, don't be stubborn,' he says. 'Have you heard the one about the guy who got caught in the flood? Everyone was rushing out of town, the flood was going to drown them. A motorcyclist stopped for him and offered him a ride. The man said, "No thanks, God will save me." The flood was up to his knees. An hour later, a car stops, the driver yells for him to jump in. Same thing: "No thanks, God will save me." Now the flood's waist deep. A truckie sees him, toots his horn, urges him, climb in. "No thanks, God will save me." Of course, the flood drowns him. When he gets to the Pearly Gates, he's a little upset. He demands God say why he wasn't saved. He was a man of faith. God says, "I sent three people, dickhead. What else did you expect?"'

I burst out laughing.

'So where do you need to go, prince?'

'Department of Births and Deaths.'

'Oh, that doesn't sound good either way. If it's birth, my commiserations for the long road ahead. If it's death, please ignore my poor sense of humour. Unless you're happy with the death, in which case I wish you a substantial inheritance.'

I like his sense of life. Anyone with no teeth and a decaying car who can laugh in a blizzard is fine by me.

'Actually,' I say, 'I need to go a few places today. So maybe you can stay with me the whole day, if you give me a good price.'

'Free,' he says.

'Nope,' I say. *Taarof*. I'm sick of it: just charge me.

'Look into my eyes,' he says.

I do as instructed.

'My eyes are happy to take you for free.'

I am still suspicious. 'Here's the thing. I've had drivers say this exact same thing, then charge me triple the fee.'

'Well, you're in luck,' he says, 'because triple zero is still zero. Come on, I'm getting cold here. And I'm getting older too. So are you going to get in or am I going to kick your ass?'

Once I'm in the car, we settle on 60,000 tomans—about $20 Australian, which seems low to me.

'Are you absolutely sure?' I say.

He keeps driving. 'The only thing I've ever been unsure about is marrying my wife.'

He gets me to the Department of Births and Deaths by six-thirty. It doesn't open till seven. I invite the man to breakfast. He accepts.

We order the usual suspects: eggs, cheese, jam, butter, bread. It's the first food I've really *tasted* in days. That's what kindness can do for you.

Once the department opens, I take a ticket and get called up first. I present a tiny man with large glasses my thrice-stamped envelope.

He opens the envelope and peers at the materials within.

'Where is his other passport?' he demands.

'What? Which?' I respond, baffled.

'His Afghan one.'

'He is not Afghan. He is Australian.'

'Why does it say he's Afghan here?'

My heart sinks.

'What? No, no, no. That can't be. He is Australian. That's what I told the lady-lieutenant.'

'You have to get this rectified,' he says. 'Go back to Foreign Affairs. Get them to issue you a new paper.'

'Sir, I'm running out of time.'

But paperwork is paperwork. My driver burns rubber.

❖ ❖ ❖

Forty minutes later, I'm back at Foreign Affairs. I shove my way to the front and feel very bad about it, but all the good feelings in the world aren't going to get me home.

I reach the female soldier I dealt with yesterday.

'Ma'am-Lieutenant. Good morning,' I say. 'You wrote that my dad is Afghan, can you please fix it up?'

'Did I?' she asks inscrutably. 'Oh, I did.'

She corrects it with liquid paper, and blows it dry. I follow her neat handwriting: 'Australian of Iraqi origin.' She stamps and dates the changes.

'Come back soon,' she says.

❖ ❖ ❖

Back at the Department of Births and Deaths, I take another number. Ticket C397. The screen's only on C289. Nearly a hundred people, and only eight windows.

Two hours later, I'm standing at one of them. It's not the same officer from before.

'Why does this have liquid paper on it?' the new officer enquires.

I explain the whole thing. 'Okay, I didn't ask for your life story,' he interrupts. 'You need a new paper from Foreign Affairs.'

'What?' I whisper, in shock.

'Who served you here?'

I find the small man with the glasses. His colleague calls him up.

'I told you to get new papers,' he tells me. 'Did I not?'

'No, sir,' I say.

'Don't *no, sir* me,' he says. 'Anyway, we can't process this. The serial numbers won't match.'

'Why won't it match?' I ask. 'Actually, here you go. I have the coroner's report, the police report, the court report, the embassy report. Will it match any of those?'

'Don't create a ruckus,' he says, 'or I'll have you kicked out. This is a legal issue, not an emotional one. See this serial number? In our system, it means your father is Afghan. It doesn't matter that they've changed what the paper says. Our computer won't process it.'

'We're letting a computer tell us what to do? We built that computer,' I say helplessly.

'Don't create a circus for us!' the man shouts. 'I told you nicely what needs to be done. The onus was on you to listen to my instructions and carry them out. And now, guess what? It's still on you to go and fix it up.'

I break down inside, but keep my head up.

'Sir,' I say. 'I'm not from here.'

'And that is not our problem,' he says. But he lowers his tone. 'You seem like an intelligent man. So go sort this out.'

'There's no way I can make it back here before closing hours.'

'Then come back Sunday.'

'My visa expires on *Saturday*.'

What can he do? He walks off.

❖ ❖ ❖

And soon, I'm face to face with the lady-lieutenant again. There is more barging that makes this happen. I still feel guilt, but not as much.

'Ma'am-Lieutenant, I need you to issue me a new paper,' I say.

'Why?' she asks.

'They didn't accept this.'

'They should have. It's been stamped.'

'They didn't,' I say simply. 'Serial number problem.'

While she's writing the new paper, and stamping it a zillion times, I break down inside just enough to start babbling out loud.

'Now I need to get back there, then get back here, to get the exit papers from you…'

'You'll need to extend your visa,' she says calmly, not looking up.

'I already have,' I say. 'I have no more extensions left.'

She gives the paper one last stamp.

'Look here,' she says. 'Take this to them, quickly, and come back ASAP.'

'What if you're closed?' I all but mewl.

'One problem at a time.'

And so I take the paper, and get back in the car, grateful for the driver, who does like to drive fast. He pushes his rust-bucket car for everything it's got. In the traffic, which does not comply with his attitude, I begin to recite the Koran under my breath. Surely things can't end like this.

◆ ◆ ◆

I march straight to the counter of the tiny man with the large glasses and drop the paper in front of him.

'Can't you see I'm serving a customer?' he barks. 'Get a number and wait your turn, this country has laws.'

'But—'

'Stop remonstrating! You're not the only one with a problem here. All these people sitting down, you see them? What do you think they're here for?'

Fair point. So, I get a ticket. But it's twenty-odd people behind, only two counters are open, and it's already three o'clock.

I start to tell my story to the people in line, and ask openly if anyone might help by giving me their number. I'm so animated, I know I'm coming across as a total loon, but I can't help it: I look possessed because I feel that way too.

A few people protest gamely, saying I should just wait my turn. Others are sympathetic, but say they've been waiting for hours, and can't risk the place closing on them.

Suddenly, another idea sprouts up.

'What if I buy your number?' I suggest. 'How much is it worth to you? I'll buy your number. Cash.'

Everyone stays quiet, so I keep pushing it.

'What's the daily wage here? Twenty thousand, thirty? I'll triple it, quadruple it. One ticket, one hundred thousand!'

I'm interrupted by the loudspeaker: the next number is called. A hunched man who looks like he was buddies with Moses gets up. He looks at his ticket, then looks at the cash in my hands. He approaches me gingerly, and speaks even slower than his walk.

'I came…all the way from…the village…to register my grandson's… birth. And if I don't…do it…there…is a fine. I will need… to come back…Sunday. And I can't…come back…on Sunday. My wife…is very…frail.'

'What's the fine?' I ask him.

'Twenty thousand.'

'So I'll pay it. And your trip back to Mashhad. Deal?'

'How about…my time…off?'

'How can you possibly be working?' I blurt. He looks like he retired before I was born.

He takes a deep breath. 'In a village…we are always… together. When I leave my…family…they get…upset. That's… our…lifestyle. And…'

'Two hundred thousand, that's my offer.'

He takes another long breath to speak, so I cut in.

'It's a lot of cash and you know it.'

'Thank you…you are very kind.'

'No. I'm just desperate,' I toss back. It's true. I'm horrified by my behaviour. But I bury this in the growing pile of things I can feel bad about later on, once my father's not in a refrigerator, and I'm on a flight back home.

'I see you buy people out,' says the small man with the large glasses.

'He was free to choose,' I mumble.

He types the details into the computer.

'Hmm. Actually, no. Can't do this,' he frowns. 'The system already has it that your father is Afghan, and it doesn't know how to accept two deaths for the one person. It's saying this man's already dead, and I can't really change it. Your only option is to get the matter overturned in court. That takes maybe two, three weeks.'

'The hell it won't,' I utter, defiant but nervous.

'Excuse me?' he blinks.

'You heard me,' I say. 'I don't even have two hours, and you're telling me two weeks. For an error that wasn't even my fault to begin with.'

'Yes, it was,' he affirms, 'and if you'd listened to me—'

'Who is your manager? I want to speak to him.' I'm almost shouting now.

'Lower your voice, sir, or I'll kick you out.'

'Fuck you, mate!' I blurt in English.

I wildly scan the room. By the stairs: a sign, manager's office. I take the paper and sprint upstairs. I make it to the door marked *Manager* before a guard stops me.

'The sheikh is in a meeting,' he says.

I think about it for an ant's time of a second. 'I don't care,' I say.

I push past the guard and barge in.

The manager is a white-bearded cleric. Gathered around the room are a bunch of young inmates in grey-striped uniforms. They are a dejected crew. He's in the middle of a moral lecture. He stops and looks up.

'Out!' he gestures.

Whatever I'm going to do, I have to do it fast.

'My father was the lead cleric in Melbourne, Australia,' I say all in a rush. He goes to interrupt, but I just keep talking. 'He passed away in the city and I am trying to get him back. I need a death certificate from this department to take to Foreign Affairs. My visa expires in two days and it's a public holiday tomorrow. I have no other option but to plead my case to you.'

He regards me for a moment. 'Why not bury him in Mashhad?' he asks.

'Sir, his family and community are all back in Melbourne.'

He inspects my attire.

'Why aren't you wearing black?'

I don't understand what he means. I look at my clothes: washed blue jeans, a charcoal jumper with a blue shirt under it. A heavy grey jacket. Then I get it. Traditionally, that's the first thing the family of the deceased do: they wear black.

'I don't know,' I stutter. 'I didn't think of it.'

He waves me off. 'I'm busy with these young criminals. Come back next week.'

'Please.'

Suddenly, he slams shut the thick book on his lap. 'Australia!' he exclaims. 'Is it good there? We hear a lot about its beaches.'

'Huh? Yes. They're good,' I tell him, baffled.

He looks alarmed. 'Why? Do you go?'

'Oh,' I say. 'No, of course not, they're a place of sin. But they are good. So I've heard.'

He eyes me apprehensively. 'Is it true women roam around naked?'

'I...think so?' I tell him. 'But as I said, I don't know.'

He reopens his book. 'Come back next week, I'll see you then. Right now, all I can see is that you have a big tongue instead.'

'Your Highness, please,' I say.

'Get out and close the door.'

The guard goes to remove me, but I give up without a fight. I've tried paying money. Being nice. Talking polite. And what's left? I'm not far off an anxiety attack; I can feel it. I've been hospitalised for blacking out before.

My stomach goes empty. My heart rate jacks up. I fight to keep my senses going.

I'm losing the fight.

Slow the fuck down, I urge my heart. I remind it who's in charge. I'm the boss. I love my dad. The chemicals can't wreck this. I have to start breathing again, just like I do in yoga.

Think of the pool.

Think how long I can hold my breath underwater.

The hours I spend underwater.

And on the football oval.

All that work has to come back now.

Steady.

Steady.

Steady, mate.

I'm snapped out of it by the sensation of a hand upon my shoulder.

It's the young soldier. 'What's wrong, brother?' he asks. 'Can I help you with something?'

I focus on my breathing. I focus on his big, dark eyes. Does he want money?

But I can't read him. I can see the whole universe in those eyes.

He feels I am about to fall, and grips my shoulder harder. He squats down in slow motion to match the pace of my drop.

He leans me against the wall, his hand still on my shoulder.

'You point your weapon at me one minute and help me in another?' It takes a while to get the words out; I'm breathing all heavy.

'That?' he says. 'That was just my job. *This*, this is my duty.'

'Thank you, brother. Thank you.'

'I haven't done anything yet,' he replies.

'I took it to the highest person here. You can't help me. It's all over.'

'Have you seen the deputy? He's a true gentleman.'

'I've already seen the cleric.'

'The deputy has just as much power. Just go in, he's a good man. A really, really good man.'

'As are you, brother.'

I place my hand on his shoulder; his is still on mine. We must look like schoolboys.

But we're not schoolboys. We're adult men. I instinctively reach for my wallet. But he grabs my hand and pushes it firmly away.

'Duty is priceless, brother. All I ask is a prayer. I'm going to be a father soon.'

My eyes light up at the news. 'Congratulations!' I tell him. 'My daughter just turned seven.'

'And how does it feel?'

'It's amazing, man. You're really going to enjoy it.' I shove a banknote in his pocket, for the child. And before he can give it back, I hurry downstairs.

❖❖❖

At 3.35 pm, I'm in the deputy's office.

He is a neatly bearded middle-aged man, wearing a thick precious-stone ring. I immediately get a great vibe from him: maybe it's the fact he's not pointing a gun at me, or maybe it's just the way, miraculously, he stops sipping his tea as soon as he notices me.

I explain my story and, thank God, he understands the problem of time. He stands up at once and yells out into the main hall, gesturing to the tiny man with the large glasses. He calls him in.

'Why are you giving this young guest of ours a hard time?' the deputy asks him.

'I didn't. He was the deaf one not hearing my instructions.'

'First of all, you just don't insult a guest like this. Second, if he made a mistake, you should show compassion and help him solve it. What is this computer-system business you've been dealing him? You can't use your head and bring the file to me so I can delete it?'

'I'm sorry, sir. I knew you were busy and I didn't want to disturb—'

'Don't tell me you're sorry. Just fix it. And while you're at it, apologise.'

The tiny man with the big glasses takes my paper and regards me. He heads out of the room and the deputy says, 'I hope you can get your father out in time.'

'Thank you, sir,' I say. 'I will never forget your humanity.'

But he's already back to his papers. He really is a busy guy.

❖❖❖

PAPERWORK IS PAPERWORK

I arrive at the Department of Foreign Affairs fifteen minutes after closing. The guard doesn't even want to let me past the checkpoint. I plead with him. I beg with him. 'Please, just call and check.'

He shrugs, picks up the phone, dials it. Nothing. 'They're gone.'

Before he can finish, I see the lady-lieutenant leaving through the gates. I scamper across to her.

'Ma'am! Ma'am-Lieutenant!' I call.

She turns to the source of the clamour and stops.

'I made it! I made it!' I cry.

'No, you didn't. We are closed,' she motions, moving on.

I stand, stock-still. 'Please, you know my story. Please!'

For one second, she stops.

She turns around slowly.

'You are keen to ruin my day, aren't you?'

❖ ❖ ❖

Ten minutes later I am in the office. The lady-lieutenant takes the death certificate—and stamps it. All is good.

She writes me an exit paper, stamps it too.

My hands are shaking.

Shaking.

The paper is no bigger than the size of my palm.

All this pain, all this trembling, for one flimsy little card.

Exit granted. Exit bloody granted.

The more I try to calm myself, the bigger the earthquakes in my brain. The lady-lieutenant leaves the office. 'Oof! You are so persistent,' she says on the way out.

I raise my voice above a whisper and wish her a very good weekend.

♦♦♦

My decrepit driver has been with me almost twelve hours, and I suggest he take his money and get back to his life. He declines. 'You still look stressed,' he says. 'So my job isn't done.'

He's right about the first part, so I let the second part lie. I ask him to take me to Reza's Paradise. I haven't seen my father since I left him for Tehran.

On the way, I'm reminded that we haven't stopped for food since our colourful breakfast, waiting for the Department of Births and Deaths to open. My poor driver's been surviving on tea and biscuits all day long.

We stop by an Iraqi restaurant—a rarity in this town. A few Iraqis greet me down a flight of stairs. The driver is taken aback. He hadn't known I was an Arab. He jokes that I have chosen the wrong old man to spy on.

This is the first time he has eaten at an Iraqi establishment in his long life. Two of his brothers were shot dead by Iraqis in the war.

'Should we leave?' I ask him.

'No way,' he replies. 'I actually want to try the same food as the men who killed my brothers. Must've been some kind of super food. They were smart, fit lads!'

TRUTH ISN'T THE BEST MEDICINE

Melbourne, Australia, 2001

Creative answering

For a seventeen-year-old Muslim boy on the Kangaroo Continent, the last year of high school and the beach were not a good match. I spent a lot of time checking out babes at the beach instead of balancing chemical equations.

As the millennium came to a close, so did my education. I collected my Year 12 results and put them in my pocket. I didn't have the guts to look at them in public.

High school wasn't all awful; I was going to miss some of it. English was mandatory, but I happened to love it. Arabic was great too, and Maths came naturally.

But I'd been barred from doing most of the subjects I really wanted: Visual Art, Performing Arts, Music and Phys Ed. These were non-starters for the Shiite Iraqi Muslim. 'Do they teach that as a *subject*?' my family said of the arts. Not only were artists rebellious outcasts who would go to hell, they also didn't have real jobs and lived in their own fairy-floss worlds. They sat on social benefits and/or swindled the taxpayers into funding whatever foolish 'vision' they'd set their hearts on next.

And so while Dad had once said, 'As doctors heal us physically, so artists heal the soul,' I was pretty sure this magnanimous theory would not apply to his own eldest son.

I did contemplate running away and becoming an artist, with a view to setting up camp in a remote locale and probably eating raw insects. But my warm bed and my mother's cooking were too much to give up.

In lieu of such drastic measures, I enrolled in Chemistry and Physics, under not-inconsiderable pressure from my family. The fortune teller had predicted that I'd become a master surgeon, and who was I to argue with fate?

And yet my aptitudes and her predictions completely failed to match up. I quite simply sucked at science subjects. When exam time rolled around, I had to resort to some creative answering.

Question 32. A compound is found to have a molecular mass of 90 atomic mass units and a simplest formula of C_2H_5O. The molecular formula of the substance is:

A. $C_3H_6O_3$
B. C_4H_26O
C. $C_4H_{10}O_2$
D. $C_5H_{14}O$

> Dear examiner,
> By now you would have notice I haven't answered much right & I'm going to fail and if I do it will have HUGE repercussions. You don't understand, if I fail, then my father fails & my father is definitely not a failure like me.
> Please also take into consideration the effects the 8-year-long Iran-Iraq war had on my upbringing, particularly my early education. ~~I want to be smart~~ It is very hard to come to a new country & new language & do yr 12. Imagine yourself in my country doing a physics or chem exam at 17 in Arabic or Farsi. ~~Please give~~ ~~miss~~. I don't want a free ticket. I'm just under insurmountable pressure to be a doctor & be smart like Dad. All the community is WAITING for my result.
>
> (cont'd overleaf.)

> Unfortunately I didn't study hard enough ~~because of edjuting to the culture of Australian beaches~~. And now I am charge of pen (sorry black pen stopped) So now I am left with begging you. Please sir/madame – you are a human being like me, your stomach fills up with a meal & you go to the toilet to empty it. So we are the same.
> I hope you are compassionate enough & have the heart to let this one slip.
> NO ONE WILL KNOW
> Thanks in advance & God be with you...

How convincing was this? I really wasn't sure, but I had to believe it was possible I'd passed. All I needed to get into Medical Science was a 98.9. I opened the envelope with a bold spirit and a light heart.

68.7.

Shit.

I walked inside the house. Mum was waiting at the door, barely containing her excitement.

'Hey, *sowmeh*! The results, the results, please! Your friend Luay got 99.2.'

My mouth was so dry I'd have paid for some saliva. 'Good, good, good, good. I'm good. Reallllly good,' I said.

'Are you okay?'

'Yes, goooood. I'm just veeeery tired from things. I will go to my rooooom and I will pray, I think. I need to pray, it's prayer time. Prayyyy!'

'So what did you get?' Mum's words fell on my mind like five little axes.

'I haven't checked. I'll check after prayer. Prayer is of utmost importance.'

I rushed to my room and closed the door, praying for an earthquake.

Not only would my results not get me into Medicine, they would make my father the laughing stock of Melbourne. He was so well educated, two PhDs to date. And this all despite a past that included having been tortured by his uncle and fleeing oppressive countries, twice. And who was I? I was a pampered boy in a pampered country, and I couldn't muster half as good a score.

Downstairs, all night, the phone rang off the hook with people calling to brag about their own children's results. In response to this, I continued to hide.

People assembled outside the mosque, just metres from our house. I could see my fellow graduates, chatting with their proud dads. I didn't really care what any of them might think of me, but Mum and Dad would have to endure something unimaginable. People would lose respect for Dad; what good was a community leader if he couldn't raise his own children? They would say so many hurtful things it already hurt.

A knock on my window. It was 99.2. It was actually my friend Luay, but the scores were so important they superseded people's names. He grinned, pressing his result sheet against the glass.

'Hey! How are you, brother? I'm off to Medical Science! Come out! Stop hiding!'

I closed the curtain on Luay and limped down to the mosque, ashen-faced on a blue, sunny day.

Our mosque, from the outside, just looked like a large square building block, which is because our mosque was just that. Inside was a different story: large halls lavishly adorned with Koranic calligraphy, chandeliers, Islamic banners and Persian carpets all spiralling out from a gorgeously carved wooden pulpit.

Another significant feature on our tour of the mosque was Dad's rival, a severe cleric named Sayyed Ghaffar, who also happened to be the father of 99.2, aka my friend Luay.

Sayyed Ghaffar wore a black turban to signify he'd descended from the Prophet (Dad, by contrast, wore white). Family trees were extremely important for anyone named Sayyed, who considered their direct link to the Prophet's blood not only a blessing but a mark of their inherent superiority. I once had to relinquish the front seat of a car to a Sayyed, who also happened to be five years old at the time.

And here Sayyed Ghaffar was now, Luay by his side. Sayyed Ghaffar had a habit of speaking very slowly, because that way you would know he was a thinker.

'Please, my dear brethren! Let us not be so vocal in praising my son for his incredible score of 99.2. It is all the work of God Almighty. It is not my genes, or endless hours of schooling that have brought upon this splendid score. It is thanks to *Him*!'

Sayyed Ghaffar dramatically cast his eyes skyward, and the assembled neighbours chanted praise in unison. When he was finished, he spotted me standing sheepishly in the background and raised a hand to halt people's ruckus.

'But wait! We must not be so joyous. Perhaps our cleric's son, Osamah, has not done so well.'

'What are you saying, Sayyed! Osamah is a top student,' a mosque-goer said. The support would have been comforting if I'd actually earned it.

Another joined in. 'Even if he slept through his exams he would be the top student! There is no man smarter than his father!'

'I would bet my entire house on Osamah getting a higher score than Luay! Of course, gambling is a sin so I will not do it.' These fighting words came from a septuagenarian. All turned their ravenous eyes towards me.

'Let us hear it then,' said Sayyed Ghaffar. 'What did you get?'

Luay was quietly watching. I suspected he knew. He knew, at least, how I was with science subjects.

Between being the cleric's son and a Sunday schoolteacher, where I gave lessons in Arabic—all that was over now, thanks to a number—I had given so many speeches in this very hall. But never had I felt so many eyes truly *on me*. Then I stopped feeling any of them, because I spotted Dad. He was walking towards us, in his traditional garb and traditional smile.

'I got ninety-nine also,' I declared. 'Point nine. I got 99.9.'

Complete silence.

Then a glorious chant erupted through the hall.

Better scores through Photoshop

Most of the speeches I had given at the mosque were about being a good Muslim, how best to follow the path of the Prophet. That, I could handle. Today, I had to give a speech about being a top student—warding my fellow youngsters off the wicked course of the West, inspiring them to be more like yours truly.

Mum was calling everyone, family in Iran, Iraq and Europe, cousins, aunts, uncles, grandparents. If she'd had the prime minister's number, she'd have used it now.

'My handsome boy is going to be a doctor,' she gushed. 'And some thought he was going to struggle to get to eighty-five. That shows them. He has his father's genes, you see…'

As I walked to the mosque, and my doom, I felt the air compress me. I ascended the pulpit and took a deep breath.

'Brothers and sisters,' I began. 'Scores should not matter. Surely we are equal. Surely what is more important is our intentions. We cannot judge somebody simply on their score.

'There is a funny saying the English have: you say potato, I say potarto. Whether I got a 99.9, or, say, sixty-odd, I'd still be the same flesh-and-blood person standing before you today.

'My heart would pump the same blood, and nothing would change. Thank you.'

Convenient, or inspiring? Potato, potarto. The community decided on the latter. I stepped down and they mobbed me like the paparazzi. I was at an epicentre of attention.

'Will you prescribe painkillers for my joints?' one asked me, as though I was already a doctor. 'Do you think you'll treat Jewish patients? How?'

Edging the crowd were Sayyed Ghaffar and Luay, conspicuously less effusive. Finally, Sayyed Ghaffar interrupted.

'We need a copy of your results, Osamah,' he said cheerily. 'Not because we doubt you! Because we want to frame them, and decorate the mosque with your glory.'

I marinated in my sweat.

'Of course, Sayyed,' I said breezily. 'I will bring it first thing.'

I was still hunched behind my PC well after midnight. I had scanned my results in a high-quality digital format, and I was photoshopping as if my life depended on it. When I was through with the results sheet, I had to create a letter of offer from the University of Melbourne.

It was dawn by the time I'd finished, and I needed to get some sleep. I deleted my temporary working files and shredded my cut-out letterheads.

But what to do with the original results sheet? I wanted to

stash it in my pillow—they were the real deal, after all—but I remembered all the crims who got caught by being sloppy.

I torched the papers in the kitchen and flushed the ashes.

Worsening woes

In the Shiite calendar, the Battle of Karbala was a significant event: the martyrdom of Imam Hussain, the third imam and son of Ali, the Prophet's successor (or fourth successor, according to the Sunnis). It's not as confusing when you study a solid thousand hours' worth of historical text.

What was confusing was that its anniversary fell at Christmas time. While the rest of Australia was stuffing stockings and glazing hams, I was giving a speech on the Battle of Karbala. The mosque had a potent, serious mood: black drapes, low lighting, paintings of Imam Hussain mid-battle. Everyone was wearing black today.

Ironically enough, my speech centred on truthfulness—how one must be truthful to oneself and fight one's inner demons before one was ready to do battle outside. I paralleled this teaching with Imam Hussain's stance against the tyrant: he went out to fight Yazid because of his beliefs and principles. He was *true* to himself and what he stood for and didn't back down, even though he knew death was the only drink he would be served.

In the end, Imam Hussain and seventy-two companions were trapped by Yazid's army in the desert of Karbala and on the tenth day of Muharram—the sacred first month of the Islamic lunar calendar—they were killed, but not defeated.

I, on the other hand, was defeated but not yet killed.

After I finished, a devout member took the mic and began a *latmia*.

A super-quick introduction on *latmia* for the uninitiated. *Latmia* comes from the Arabic word *latom*, which means literally 'to beat'. We beat our chests, lightly to severely, when a *latmia* is chanted. The *latmia*'s verses have a staccato rhythm, and the congregation moves as one with the movements of the notes, beating themselves on the chest to mourn the martyrdom of Imam Hussain.

This is a *latmia* in theory.

In practice, some of us younger boys wore singlets and shirts and beat ourselves to show everyone we were super devout. The harder you hit yourself, the more devout you looked. Since there was also a live feed transmitting everything into the female section, we used this opportunity to show off our pumped biceps and chests. Knowing we would appear on the flat-screen TVs, we hit ourselves all the harder and more passionately in the hope that we'd look both devout and ripped.

On this day, I beat myself so hard I numbed both my chest and hands. A month after my 'acceptance' to the University of Melbourne, I still hadn't been found out. Instead of the customary hymn, 'Hussain, Hussain', I was chanting 'idiot, moron'. Some members thought I was so in the zone they stepped back to admire me beating my lanky body senseless.

I drove to the 7-Eleven, where I'd been working for a while—to pay for my acting courses, and to distract me from my woes. I had to get into Medicine, and I did not know how. I concocted a new plan as I drove.

Faking Your Medical Degree in Eight Easy Steps
1. Score enough to do an Arts degree.
2. Enrol.
3. Pretend you're enrolled in Medicine.
4. Love Arts; therefore, get High Distinctions.
5. Leverage these. Enrol in Medical Science.
6. Work your butt off in Medical Science like you should've done in high school.

7. Armed with a BA in Medical Science and a great GAMSAT score, apply for Medicine. Get in.
8. Twelve years later, become a doctor. Figure out whether and how you will treat Jewish patients.

If anybody asked why it was taking me so long, I'd just tell them I was 'specialising' or something.

First things first: I'd been so engrossed in my scheming that I hadn't noticed the flashing blue and red lights behind me. I pulled over.

'Good evening, sir. Any reason why you ran a stop light back there?'

'Did I?'

'Is this your vehicle?'

'Huh?'

'Is this your car?'

'Yeah, nah, mate.' I flashed my best, most pious smile.

'Have you got your licence on you?'

I did have my licence on me. But I was still on my L-plates. This was embarrassing. I'd turned eighteen two weeks ago, but I'd also failed my driving test. I was a fake top student who'd been accepted into a fake degree, and I was a fake legal driver too.

I handed the cop my learner's permit and read a verse from the Koran, hoping it would scramble his vision, Jedi mind trick–style. It didn't. It never does.

'You're unlicensed, mate.'

'Technically.'

'What do you mean technically? You're on your L-plates.'

'Yeah, nah, but I know how to drive.'

'Any reason why you're driving unlicensed?'

'I have to get to work.'

'Any reason why you've failed to display your L-plates?'

That was an easy one. 'If I put on my L-plates then you'd know I was an L-plater. Can't give it away that stupidly.'

He looked at me Clint Eastwood–style, ducked back to his car, and came back with two $500 fines and a court notice. 'Do not drive this car again,' he warned.

I waited six minutes so he was completely gone before cranking up the engine.

At the 7-Eleven, I put my name badge on—*Sam*—and took over for the night shift.

Most nights, around 2 am, a few young Muslim boys came into the servo to keep me company, loitering deep into the night. One of them was the member who'd read the *latmia* at the mosque. He was very devout, had a longer beard than all of us combined, and wore a green shawl to mark that he, too, was a Sayyed.

'You beat your chest good tonight,' he said approvingly. 'You've gained great heavenly rewards. Is that a new issue of *Hustler*?'

Normally, Sayyed liked to read them alone in the staff toilets, because he wanted to conduct 'research on how to have sex'. After he'd come out, the colour leaping off his face, I'd reseal the magazines using a lighter.

Young Sayyed took his *Hustler*, and I took up the mop and bucket and began my nightly cleaning duties. As I scrubbed, I wished there was a cleaning system for the mind—some *Men in Black*–type device to wipe your whole hard drive. Alas, the best I could do was shine the floors until they sparkled and wonder how I was supposed to drive home.

INSHALLAH

Mashhad, Iran, 2013: one day until visa expires

Reza's Paradise is closed when my driver and I arrive there after dinner, so I thank him liberally for his time and tip him three times more than the quoted price. It's the best money I've spent all week. He's sixty-seven years old, and he kicked me around this enormous city like a piece of clockwork. Thanks to him, I have the exit paper. I am indebted to his soul.

It's three in the morning, and accommodation is a no-go. So I seek refuge at Reza's shrine. At least my father's nearby. I leave my luggage in the allocated spot and walk in as a pilgrim. There are guards whose job it is to keep such pilgrims awake, so I haven't been able to sneak any shut-eye. But I'm away from the snow outside. It is warm and cozy.

◆ ◆ ◆

My visa expires tomorrow, so when the sun comes up today, I need to finish two more urgent tasks. First, I must get Dad's body sorted at Reza's Paradise; Australia won't accept him unless he's been embalmed to 'international standards'.

Second, my passport—that handy thing—is still at the cemetery, and I'm not sure how much longer I can keep getting by with my swim pass.

Today is Friday, which is the weekend in Iran. Getting a plane ticket for me—not to mention one for Dad—out of Iran tomorrow will be tough work. Finding an open travel agent that has two tickets at such late notice…just the thought of it makes me nauseous.

I take deep breaths and try to think of the worst-case scenario.

If I can't get a ticket to Australia, I'll get a ticket *out of Iran*—any destination will keep me out of jail tomorrow. Once I'm in whatever country will have me and my dad, I can try to get us home to the Kangaroo Continent from there.

At 5.30 am, I pray and leave the shrine, knowing this—inshallah—will be my last time here. If I have another opportunity, it'll be because I'm stuck in Iran, and everything I've done so far will have vanished into the air.

◆ ◆ ◆

I arrive at Reza's Paradise at 7 am. It seems an eternity since I was last here, a trick embellished by the fact that the lady who refused to hand back my passport isn't there this morning. A different clerk asks me to pay the fee before they can proceed to prepare the body.

As I pay, I realise this is pretty much the last of my money. I have just enough Iranian currency to pay the storage fee and get me back to the city. I don't want to think about how many cabs I've caught this week. Nor about the fact that banks here are closed on the weekends.

At the charnel-house, the young man whose job is to 'prepare' the body invites me in so I can help him move my dad.

A silent scream rips through me. I haven't seen Dad in days. It feels like years, even, and I still haven't accepted he is gone. The young man drags the black sack out of the refrigerated room. He unzips it, but I don't need to look at Dad's calm, cold, resting face. I can tell from the thick black hair who the body is.

'God rest his soul. He's been washed and put in a shroud as you asked.'

I don't reply.

'Now pull him with me, on three.'

He counts and on three we lift Dad and haul him outside, setting him down beside a wooden box.

'This box looks small,' I say.

'No brother, it's perfect.'

'He'll get squeezed in.'

'That's a solid box. It won't hurt him, brother, I promise.'

His tone is calm and true. It eases my anxiety a hair tip's per cent. 'On three,' he says. And we lift my dad and place him in the box.

I suffocate looking at it.

'He will be okay, brother,' the man says. 'Now I am going to put some chemicals on his body, eyes and face, so maybe you are going to want to step outside.'

❖ ❖ ❖

At 1 pm, the cab pulls over by the sixth travel agent we've tried since leaving Reza's Paradise. This one is closed too.

I press the driver: the next one, please.

He tells me to come back looking again on Monday.

Fed up with the negativity, I leave the cab and hail another.

But all the other cabbies are telling me the same thing: I won't find an open travel agent today or tomorrow.

At my fourth refusal, I ask one of the drivers if he won't take me to *every single travel agent in the entire town*. And if he's right and I'm wrong, I'll look very foolish and he'll still have the money from driving this foolish guy around.

He thinks about it, nods, and drives me directly to the national airline carrier's authorised agent. He tells me this is the only one with a remote chance of being open. This is what it boils down to. This is the last one.

I drag my luggage across the road.

It's closed too, of course.

I drop Dad's suitcase, chuck the guitar on top and let go of the walking stick.

The cabbie is long gone, and every shop is closed. I stand alone in the middle of the silent, empty road, a backpack glued to my back, surrounded by the rubble of my long, quixotic quest. I do a 360-degree spin, don't notice my surroundings. It's all a blur. I look up. The clouds are laughing violently.

Then I look back at the closed shop. Another trick of the eye? Or is there someone moving in there? I adjust my focus.

An old lady behind the door is putting on her chador, busying herself by the door, ready to leave the office.

I pick up my rubble and tear across the road. I bang on the window frantically. Startled, she freezes.

I try to force the door open but it's locked from the inside. I bang on it like a madman. She gestures, 'We are closed.' She's clearly terrified.

Desperate, I start knocking harder and shaking the door, shouting and crying, 'Emergency…please open…emergency.'

As I bang in a frenzy, my hands suddenly lock. Then I feel a kick to the back of my knees and I slump to the ground.

A big-boned, thick-moustached, middle-aged man sits on top of me, landing a blow to my face.

'What do you want with my wife?' he yells.

I try to protest, but he's squashing my airways.

'Why are you here at this hour?'

He sinks his knee deeper into my stomach. I wheeze in pain.

'Did you know she was coming to work? Is that why you're here?'

Finally, he lets some pressure off. 'I'm here to buy a ticket! I can't breathe!'

'What ticket? This place is closed. It's Friday! You son-of-a-bitch liar, you!'

'If this place is closed then what is that woman doing in the shop?'

'You tell me.'

The woman rushes out and shouts around: 'Call the police! Call the police!' But the road is dead as ever, except for this mess right here. I stop struggling—I can maybe use his weight to my advantage. I take a few breaths, go limp, and my mind comes alive. All it takes is an open-handed strike to the throat and he's on the ground.

'I'm not here for your wife,' I pant. 'My father has passed away. I am not from here. I want a ticket.'

The woman kneels over her big husband, yelling hysterically for help. She's shaking uncontrollably. 'Murderer! Murderer!' she yells.

Her husband raises a hand, very much alive, and grabs her shaking hands. 'Wait, wait,' he says, struggling to breathe. 'I think this young man does just want a ticket.'

❖ ❖ ❖

The lady had come to collect some belongings she'd left behind at the office; her husband had been sitting in his car, waiting to collect her, before the lunatic had come knocking and he'd rushed out to her aid.

She can't book a ticket for me, she regretfully explains. 'The systems are asleep. Even if they were open, your dad will need a special "cargo ticket", which no travel agent has.'

Things are looking dark again. Then she lights up my sky. She hands me the name of the sole cargo-only agent in Mashhad. And what do you know? Cargo moves around the clock. So they're open weekends.

I want to kiss both the lady and her husband, open-mouth.

FAKING IT

Melbourne, Australia, 2002

My first (and fake) day of university

My family assembled outside the house, forming an honour guard to wave me off into the world—their very own future doctor.

Mum held an ornamental bowl filled with water and tossed it at my feet. A blessing. My stomach turned.

It was my first day at university in my fake degree.

I had not enrolled in an Arts degree; three years seemed like plenty of time for people to get suspicious. Instead of this, I thought I might study in the library, sit in on lectures (no one checked the roll there), study my atoms off and try to take an admissions exam in a year's time. But the truth was, I had no real plans beyond boarding the tram.

I disembarked at the University of Melbourne and joined the throng of actual students, willing myself to be one of them as they converged upon the grounds.

Among them was Luay, who had not bothered maintaining the polite pretence that I'd been admitted to my degree.

He waved at me, in a facade of friendliness. 'How?' he asked me. 'I just want to know how. How did you get here?'

'The number 19 tram, bro.'

'I will get to the bottom of this,' he seethed. 'I worked my backside off trying to get here. You did nothing, and everyone thinks you're the real deal. They'll find out you're not, though, and when they do, I'll be watching.'

What's worse, I ask you, than having an enemy like Luay? Having an enemy like Luay who is totally, completely accurate in everything he thinks about you.

He kept his gaze steady as he melted off into the crowd, ready to make friends with people who belonged there—people like him.

I, on the other hand, was prepared to be a loner. No witnesses, no one who might sniff me out—and, of course, no one I might injure with my elaborate charade. I peeled off and headed for the library. I had books to read.

Hiding Usher in the Koran

The trouble with an eighteen-year-old boy deciding to be a loner is that eighteen-year-old boys are never really alone. Not when they can chat online. That's how I met Sisi, who was still in Year 12. She said she wanted to be a doctor.

This was the perfect opportunity to complain about my 'degree'. *People introduce me as doctor-Osamah this and doctor-Osamah that*, I complained. *I just want to scream, I'm moron-Osamah!*

You're too funny, she typed.

Please don't say that. It ends bad.

Gotta go, she typed. *Are you gonna be here later?*

Of course I would be. I was online every night. After a long shift in the library, then another at the 7-Eleven, I would look forward to chatting with her long into the night.

Her interests included scripture *and* sports. How cool was that? Polar-bear cool. She played cricket; she even knew how to bowl without bending her elbow. And she was good enough to play basketball at state level, only the religious barriers meant she could never take part in games. I was desperate to get in the nets with her and have a tonk.

When she told me she was 'Mooz' and explained it was slang for Muslim, I went around for days introducing myself as Osamah the Mooz.

The only trouble was, we weren't the same kind of Muslim.

Sisi was of Lebanese heritage, and her dad was of the view that Iraqis were the nucleus of all the Middle East's problems. My mother, for her part, was of the view that the Lebanese had ruined Middle Eastern food, which was almost as serious an allegation.

When she told me she liked Usher, I froze. Wasn't music a sin? I didn't speak to her for days while digesting it. Then I stopped playing *Age of Empires*—the greatest game on earth—long enough to start amassing a secret stash of CDs: Foo Fighters, Nirvana, Red Hot Chili Peppers, Will Smith, Sixpence None the Richer, and Usher too.

I applied stickers to their cases showing passages from the Holy Koran and hid them in plain view.

April Fool

The funny thing about a life of fraudulence and deception is that even this kind of slapdash existence eventually settles into a routine. Before I knew it, I was three months into a strange but peaceful existence: get up, catch tram, pretend to go to uni, go instead to the library and study what I can. Work at the 7-Eleven then head home and chat to Sisi, talk about our secret music. Get up. Do it all again.

Luay was still up my backside about the results, and his attempts to catch me out were getting increasingly cartoonish. It would've been embarrassing if it wasn't also kind of scary. High-school data is publicly available, provided you have the student number and the date of birth. Thankfully, nobody knew my real birthday, least of all Luay. My passport said December, but I was really born in March. Most of our documentation had been destroyed during the war, and when we'd come to Australia, Dad had bumped me up a few months so I could skip primary school.

But Luay kept running up to me when he saw me around campus, asking why he'd never once seen me in a tutorial, and who my tutors were. Finally, I approached a bald man crossing the street in view of Luay, and I asked him politely if he'd mind nodding his head at me.

'What?' he said.

'Please, sir. Huge favour. Nod your head?'

He smiled politely, declined and hurried off, which I dare say was even more convincing for my purposes. As he walked off, probably thinking I was crazy, I raised a hand and yelled, 'Thank you, professor! Now I understand.'

I turned around and grinned at Luay. Instant tutor.

But the whole process was exhausting, and getting more so by the day. With 1 April coming up, I considered taking advantage of the auspicious date, revealing the lie to my family and yelling 'April Fool!' I thought I might claim the whole thing as an elaborate practical joke, and implore them to appreciate my commitment to the gag.

All the while, I was finding ways to make Sisi love and loathe me.

I'm going crazy with school, I typed.

You have to chill out, Osamah.

Maybe I do, but if so, I'm only hot because of you.

She'd pretend to log out, but I could see she'd read my message.

DaKoolGuy83: Get it? Chill? Like, because I'm feeling hot… Hello? You there?

DaKoolGuy83: Hello?

DaKoolGuy83: Yellow?

DaKoolGuy83: Red? Blue?

Sisi and the Bombers

The day Essendon played the West Coast Eagles at Colonial Stadium in May, I applied the last layers of gel to my hair, wrapped myself up in my Bombers scarf, and got out of the house before Mum could foist Moe Greene and Ali on me.

'But you always take them with you!' she yelled as I bolted out the door.

Of course I always took them with me—they were Moe Greene and Ali. But today was the first day I was getting to meet Sisi.

I waited near Gate 3, as agreed, feeling jumpy. She'd never sent me a photo, but we'd been talking for four months. I thought I would just *know* it when I saw her.

I was wrong about so much, but it turned out I was right on this one. She was a beautiful girl with long, straight blonde-brunette hair, blue jeans and a cardie. We locked eyes. I knew it was her; she knew it was me. There are some things you can't fake, and if you're lucky, you don't need to. Sisi was a knockout, and I was one lucky—no, triple-lucky—dude.

'Hello!' I said. I didn't even try to act cool. 'I like your jumper.'

'Oh, thanks. It's a cardigan,' she said. 'How are you?'

'Um. Dazzled.' I flashed her a smile, doing my best to be just as dazzling. She cast her eyes downwards. A crowd of footy fans marched by, yelling, 'Carn ya Dons!' and cursing.

'So, Osamah who barracks for the Bombers and likes to pray,' she said. 'Do you want to go watch the game, or do you feel like walking around the stadium seven times for pilgrimage?'

We chose the game, and it passed like a dream. It was funny: I just wasn't nervous.

As soon as we got home, we both jumped online to dissect the whole experience. We were still Osamah and Sisi, same as always, thank God.

Let's go to a movie. An action movie, she said. *I grew up around boys.*

I grew up around girls, so I'd rather go dress shopping, I typed.

And then, we listened to the same Usher song quietly on our headphones, trading instant messages about how the song made us feel. Despite the distance, I felt so connected I was tingling.

At the movies, we were closer. It was like an electric shock. I remembered the times I'd tried to sneak into the cinemas in Iran. This time, I was free and I was actually *with* Sisi, even if Mum thought I was at the library studying, and even if Sisi thought I was enrolled in a Medical Science degree.

'Suck on a fat cock and choke in cum!' yelled a Mafia wiseguy.

Johnny Butterknife calmly withdrew a large kitchen knife from his jacket and slid it through the wiseguy's throat.

'How about you check if there are any cocks in hell, you motherfucking wiseguy,' he whispered, 'and gag on a bouquet of dicks while you burn?'

Action movies.

Even with the awkward dialogue, which was great, but not romantic, our arms were inching closer and finally, we were touching, skin to skin.

How could we have gone back to our bedrooms after that? When the credits rolled, we snuck quickly into another cinema, screening *Swordfish*. No sooner had we sat down than an actress started giving Hugh Jackman a blow job under the desk.

I pretended to check the time. I pretended to check my nails. I didn't want to come across as a guy who liked that kind of thing. When I looked back up, Halle Berry was baring her breasts, magnified times a hundred on the screen.

This was not a good situation. Casually as possible, I put the popcorn on my lap.

More hoping to distract Sisi than anything else, I moved my hand onto her thigh. She tensed up for a second, but made no move to reproach me. Actually, she let me keep it there for the whole film.

Arranging marriage

Q. Guess what kind of person is ripe for an arranged marriage in the eyes of a small Muslim community in Melbourne's inner north?

A. A top student who's studying to be a doctor.

The community was on all of our cases about getting married. After all, marriage supplied the other half of a person's religion. Eighteen was a 'dangerous age', especially in the Wild, Wild Tempting West, and therefore the perfect time to complete one's practice.

Combine that with the academic proof that you'll become a worthy husband, and believe me, the pressure quickly starts to mount.

One night, I came home from my secret life at the library and before I could rush upstairs to chat to Sisi, Dad showed me a grainy photo of a different young girl.

'What do you think?' he asked, eyes twinkling.

'She's sort of alright,' I mumbled.

And that's how I consented to an arranged marriage with Yomna.

FAKING IT

◆ ◆ ◆

Once this process gets started, it all happens very fast.

That same afternoon, I was squeezed into a suit and then onto a couch at Haj's, a respected member of our community. Dad was on one side of me; Haj was on the other. Two of Haj's elder sons sat on another sofa, quiet but on guard. Mum was the only woman present, on the other side of the room. There were a few community elders, prayer beads in their hands. One of them was Abu Ghazi, our resident octogenarian.

'How the cleric's son has managed to stay single this long is beyond me,' he said. 'At twenty-one I had three wives. I understand this is Australia and the laws make it tricky—still, I'm sure you'll get around to your second soon. Anyway, that's later. You must take care of the first. I am in my eighties and I still make the effort each morning to tell my wife how wonderful her breakfast was.'

Abu Ghazi had divorced his first wife, and the third had died in her sixties. His surviving wife was his second—'not my favourite, by any means', he was fond of saying.

'There is no shame in telling your wife your feelings,' he went on. 'Do not let anyone try to convince you these romantic gestures are empty. I once even told my wife'—he paused for effect, and to cough—'the dead one, I mean, that I really liked her company.

'My first wife once asked me: "Abu Ghazi, if there was a flood here and you could only rescue one of us, who would you choose?"

'I naturally replied: "I cannot choose. It is forbidden. In Islam a man must treat all his wives equally, and show them the same amount of affection."

'Still, she pressed me. "My dear wife," I told her, "you are all my wives. Besides, we are in Karbala. The desert! How could anyone imagine a flood in such a place? It will never happen!"

'As it turned out, this was a mistake on my part: she reminded me that Noah's Ark had happened. "So tell me, Abu Ghazi!" she said. "Tell me! If there was a flood here and you had to choose between us, who would you save?"

'I looked at her for a minute, with all her wrinkles. I looked at my youngest wife, so pretty. Then I turned to my oldest wife and said, "But darling, you know how to swim, don't you?"'

The room erupted with laughter, especially from the elders, who all began convulsing with a bout of synchronised coughing. Without further ado, Dad and Haj took over. It was their solemn task to read the ceremonial engagement vows.

There is really no easy way out of an arranged marriage. If I'd declined the grainy photo of Yomna, they'd only have whipped out another. Most of my friends from the mosque had already been married off last year.

Once the vows were over, Dad said, 'You are quiet.'

Mum cried, 'My boy is speechless with joy!' I could almost hear the international calls she was rehearsing in her head, and sure enough, tonight she'd be all over the phone. *My doctor son is getting married!*

'You liked her?' Dad double-checked.

'Um, I didn't see her,' I said.

'You saw the photo,' Dad said.

'It was a pretty grainy photo.'

'It was a bad angle,' said Mum. 'But she's beautiful. Also, I thought you'd be single forever.'

They kept pressing me to tell them I was happy, poking and feeling around for an answer I just couldn't give them. Eighteen didn't seem very young to them; Mum had married Dad when she was sixteen.

While they talked over me, happy and bubbly—and maybe, under the surface, a little worried—I lost myself in my own thoughts, swimming around for something to say. Most of all, I wanted to get home and talk this all over with Sisi. She would probably see the funny side of it. She might even be able to help me.

'My degree,' I blurted.

They stopped talking. 'What?' Mum said.

'It's…my degree. How can I be a proper husband while I'm studying?'

Mum squinted. 'Osamah, your dad fought in a war, studied for two decades and fathered five children all at once.'

'How can you father five children all at once? That would be very impressive. But Mum, I'm not as good as Dad. I really need to focus.'

'You are right,' said Dad.

Mum and I both looked at him with the same surprised expression.

'This is Australia. No one does more than one thing at a time. There will be too many distractions.' He thought for a minute. 'Perhaps I could convince Haj and the witnesses to hold off on the announcement. Till the end of your first year?'

'Hmm. And I'd still be engaged?' I asked in a hopeful voice.

'Of course. Congratulations!'

'Look at my boy,' said my mother. 'So eager to tell everyone he's getting married.'

Mum and Dad locked eyes over my head, and beamed at each other.

Falling in love

I wasn't going to feel about the girl in the photo the way Mum and Dad felt about each other. But still, the kinds of looks they gave each other were hardly mysterious to me. They were the kinds of looks I shared with Sisi every time we hung out.

A week after my engagement, we sat on a bench at the Royal Botanic Gardens. My impending marriage should've been pulsing in the back of my brain, but it wasn't. Instead, I was thinking about Sisi—I couldn't help it. Was it time to kiss her yet?

We'd been making small talk for the last three hours. I didn't know what was a signal and what wasn't; when I was with her, everything felt electric. Eventually, I just leaned in naturally. She leaned in too, and then we were kissing. It sounds undramatic, but that's because it felt right. This was how life was meant to be lived. It was love. I knew it.

As for everything going on back in the life I was stuck with? I'd bought myself a year to sort it out so, for now, I thought: fuck it.

Ringing in the engagement

On the sixth anniversary of my family's arrival in Australia, I went shopping for an engagement ring. What a way to celebrate! Yippee, yahoo, hooray.

For a month now, I'd used every excuse I could think of to avoid meeting Yomna. I didn't care if she turned out to be Miss Universe: I just plain didn't want her. It wasn't her fault, and there was nothing she could do about it, either. But today, there was no real getting around it.

I recognised her brother from the mosque when he pulled up in his Ford Falcon. He nodded hello, hands not moving from the steering wheel.

The passenger door opened, and out came an incredibly beautiful woman. She smiled at me, shy, then greeted me in Arabic, barely audible. '*Salam Alaikum.*'

'G'day,' I mumbled in English. 'And *Alaikum Salam,* of course.'

'Nice to meet you, my husband,' she continued in English.

'You too,' I wheezed out.

And with that, I turned from her and walked stiffly into the jewellery store. Maybe I could treat this as a chance to turn her off.

I pointed at the cheapest rings and enthused about them, hoping she'd go home and tell her family she didn't want this cheap bastard. Sadly, she praised me for being focused on the future and cleverly saving for our long life ahead.

The shop owner, a mosque member, was extremely unhelpful. 'The son of the cleric!' he said. 'You're in for a massive discount, my friend.'

Good news, I didn't even have to pay upfront. I felt sick.

Yomna took a respectful time choosing the right ring for herself. I grabbed one at random and got out of there quick as I could.

My temporary marriage

The thirteenth of October was Sisi's birthday, but we both got a present. We got each other a temporary marriage.

Sisi had been increasingly beset by a simmering sense of sin ever since our kiss in the Botanical Gardens, and she'd told me our improper coupling couldn't keep going like this. Luckily, I'd listened to those imams back in Iran, at least where girl-centric loopholes were concerned. The temporary marriage wasn't practised much down under, but Abu Ghazi, the octogenarian Casanova, was a notable fan. 'It's just like a taxi,' he'd been known to sigh happily. A time-locked marriage: you kept the meter running.

I tried to convince Sisi of the concept's validity. She'd never even heard of it, and balked at the notion that marriages could be both proper and short-lived.

'We're in Australia,' I said. 'Most marriages here are temporary.'

Eventually, I'd showed her enough scriptural evidence that she seemed at least provisionally convinced.

So on her birthday, as we stood at Brunswick Station, Platform 2, I finally popped the question. 'Do you feel like marrying me for a bit?'

My ears were ketchup-red. She nodded.

'Um, I need you to say it out loud,' I said. 'It's part of the vows.'

'Yes, I do,' she said awkwardly.

I handed her the real present. I couldn't afford more than her favourite perfume, but I'd embellished the gift with a book of ten handwritten poems.

'And will you accept these as your dowry?'

'Okay.'

'Um, I think you have to say yes again.'

'Okay. I mean, yes. I do.'

We smiled at each other. We must've looked like a couple of dorks.

'Oh!' I said. 'How long do you feel like marrying me for?'

'Hmm,' she said. 'I don't know, actually. How long were you thinking?'

'A hundred years.'

'Let's try a hundred days and take it from there.'

A hundred days! 'Really?' I said.

'Really.'

We kissed a little bit more often after that, proper and honest.

Trying to put Yomna off marrying me

Honest in the eyes of God, at least. My other wife-to-be was another story.

Later that same week, I was sitting next to Yomna at my house, the first time we'd been allowed to be alone together. It was supposed to be an exciting day.

Here was this perfectly nice, perfectly beautiful woman, behaving her best, and not a thing she could do would've made me want her. And then there was me, sweaty and bothered, and behaving like a tool—yet it seemed like nothing I could do would make her back out of the engagement. I was depressed for both of us.

'Listen, Yomna,' I said. 'I want you to know that I just don't like children. Also, I want to be an actor, which means we'll be broke for the rest of our lives. And if I ever get cast as a fat character, I'm going full-on, full-on fat. I'll eat unhealthily on purpose and die of heart disease in my youth.'

She poured me tea with three sugars, stirred them in and smiled. 'And when I put this much sugar in your tea, I'm trying to give you diabetes,' she said. 'So basically, it sounds like we're both great people.'

I had to chuckle; I couldn't help it, despite my mood. Trouble is, I'd already found a girl with a sense of humour.

Detective Dad

I arrived back from the beach on a glorious November day. I'd studied in the library all morning, but I'd made enough headway, and some guys from the cafeteria were going so I tagged along. Dad was on the couch reading when I walked through the door.

'How was uni?'

'Good! Good,' I said. It was true, almost: the textbooks were getting easier by the day, and I felt like I was actually learning something.

Dad raised his eyebrows.

'But could be better,' I added, for a little bit of realism. What kind of student admits that they like uni?

'You were just at uni then?'

My flesh blanched, as pale as cauliflower. How did Dad know? *Relax*, I thought. *Dad doesn't know.*

'Yeah,' I said casually.

'Huh. A concerned community member rang me up and said he was in his taxi when he witnessed you at a place not consistent with your religion. He was also of the firm belief that you were actually not enrolled. Is this person lying?'

I knew who 'this person' might be. And even though he was right, it galled me that my dad could possibly believe him.

'I don't know if this person's lying, but he's certainly wrong,' I said.

'So you wouldn't mind if I came to speak to your dean today.'

My turn to cock an eyebrow.

'It's still, what, 2 pm? We can make it with plenty of time. I'll even shout you dinner on Sydney Road afterwards.'

'Mmm,' I muttered. This was the most enthusiastic consent that I could muster.

In the car, Dad enthused about my impending marriage, because fate was determined today to turn him into an all-purpose instrument of torture. I squirmed in the passenger seat as he chatted away about how happy he was that I was getting married in the mosque. Between the two families, they'd invited about a thousand people. He wanted me to write a speech for all my fellow youngsters to show how great it felt to be engaged.

Sure, Dad! I wanted to say. *Can I borrow a pen?* I would then use this pen to stab myself.

At 3.40 pm, I was walking him through the campus. We passed a librarian; we passed a guard. Both of them smiled at me and said hello.

Seeing me so comfortable in the space, familiar with these people, I could sense Dad's suspicions draining away.

Unfortunately, I was not besties with the dean of the Medical School, yet we were death-marching towards this person's office right now.

First, there was the receptionist to deal with. I wondered if I could possibly use this to my advantage—could I whisper to this stranger, wink, get her to play along? It was too risky. Dad was standing right beside me.

I stood before the desk and asked to see the dean. 'Could you tell him one of his students is here please.'

She looked at me blankly. 'You mean tell *her*?'

I cleared my throat and nodded my head like a baboon. 'Yes, obviously that is what I mean. Good day to you.'

Dad and I sat down in the reception hall and waited. He started chatting about totally trivial matters: whether cricket season had started, how many batsmen I'd bowled out to date, why a batsman could be stumped by a wide delivery but not a no ball, since they were both sundries. To my own horror, I mentally begged him to start talking about the wedding—that way, I could've distracted myself with a different breed of dread.

'I'm sorry,' said the receptionist. 'The dean's gone home for the day. Can you come back tomorrow?'

I allowed my heart to flutter.

'I think we're good here. Thanks!' Dad said.

As we walked back to the car, he said, 'I don't know what's wrong with Sayyed Ghaffar; he's a very strange guy.'

And then he bought me dinner, which I pretended to enjoy while my stomach filled with a bottomless shame.

MARKET TRADING

Mashhad, Iran, 2013: one day until visa expires

I arrive at 3.30 pm.

The cargo office is closed.

I spot a mobile number in the window. I dial.

'Yes?' The man is gruff-voiced.

'Is this Keyhan Cargo? I have an emergency. I need a ticket to Australia.'

'How much luggage do you have to send?'

'It's not exactly luggage.'

'We only do freight.'

'It's my father. He's passed away. I need to get him out.'

'Why Australia? Rest his soul, by the way, and condolences, but why Australia?'

'I am an Australian citizen, so…'

'Okay. We won't open till later tonight, so come back at seven, eight.'

'But my visa expires tomorrow. I don't have that much time.'

'I said come *tonight*, at seven, eight. What does tomorrow have to do with anything? Your father will be out of here by then.'

'Really? You can get him out?'

'For the right fee, we can move ghosts. Just come back tonight.'

'Wait, wait. I've run out of Iranian money.'

'We accept dollars.'

'Australian?'

'American only.'

I think quick. 'It's trading stronger than American.'

No reply.

'The banks are closed today *and* tomorrow.'

No reply. Last bets, now.

'Maybe you know where I could find a black-market exchange?'

'Don't even think about it, kid. We have a machine in the office and we run every note under blue light.'

'The Aussie dollar is good,' I blurt. 'It's really, really good money.'

'Not in the world we live in. Good luck.'

He hangs up.

❖ ❖ ❖

At 4.15 pm, a cabbie finds me a bureau that opens for a half-day, usually till one or two, he says. When we get there, the exchange is open. Thank Noah. I walk in.

'Good afternoon,' I smile.

'Not trading today.'

'Why? You're open.'

'We're counting money.'

'What?'

'Excuse me, sir, just leave the premises.'

'No, you're open. I need money exchanged. I have a lot of it, please.'

'Just get out.'

'Where can I exchange money today?'

'I don't know. Leave, thank you.'

The man has so much money in front of him; I can see it on the desk. 'Please,' I say. 'It's not hard. Australian for Iranian. It's so easy. So, so easy. So easy to do.' I wave my Australian bills at him, demonstrating how such an exchange might take place.

'I'll call security if you don't leave at once.'

I close my eyes, and take a deep breath, and prepare my story. I wonder if this is how my father used to feel before a story: he'd come up against an obstacle, and use a parable to beat it down. He's become my parable so many times since he died; I wonder if he'd have been proud of this. It feels exploitative.

'My father has passed away,' I begin.

The teller cuts me off. 'Sorry for your father's loss but we are not trading today.'

I climb into the cab and ask if there's *anything* else open. He shakes his head, and I get to thinking for a long, long minute. Long enough for the driver to smoke two cigarettes and grind them out.

❖ ❖ ❖

It's a funny world: any city as strictly regulated as Mashhad is the kind of place that's always going to have its black markets. Being the kind of place that's always going to have its black markets, the authorities will always act strictly to shut those markets down. And since that makes a place like Mashhad a city that's strictly regulated…now isn't the time for thinking in this circular logic.

What it means, in practice, is that if the cops catch me, they will confiscate my money and I'll be left flat broke. I've seen cops raid a street like this and take everybody's money—everyone's, including the poor foreigners, who then must undertake a legal process as labyrinthine as this one.

I've therefore left my money in the boot of the cab, buried as deep in my luggage as possible. I've also written down the number plate of the cab, which hardly makes it less risky—but it's still less risky than trying my luck with the police.

I pass shady guys who all murmur 'exchange' in hushed tones.

'What's the exchange rate?' I ask one.

'For American, two thousand six hundred.'

'I have Australian.'

'Same.'

'Australian is stronger.'

'Same.'

Another dealer approaches me. 'Australian, you say?'

He grinds his teeth, all greedy: 'Two thousand five hundred.'

'I've been exchanging at three thousand three hundred all month.'

'Okay, I can do that for you,' he agrees, fluidly.

'Uh…actually, no thanks.'

'But my money is legit!' he calls after me. 'I'll go higher if you like!'

I might have foreign ways now, but I still grew up here.

Two dodgy youngsters conceal their mouths and noses with scarves. I have no choice but to keep trying my luck with people like this.

'What do you have?' one enquires.

'I have a face and you can see it. Show me yours or I'll walk.'

'Maybe I have a deformed face.'

'Better than a deformed soul. It won't bother me,' I respond, standing tall.

Maybe my body language does it; they both remove their scarves. They are two clean-shaven men, around my age.

'So, what have you got?' one says.

'Australian.'

'I can give you two thousand eight hundred. That's the best anyone can offer you, I guarantee that.'

'Three thousand, at least! I've been exchanging at three thousand three hundred.'

'You're pushing your luck on a public holiday.'

'But I have a lot to exchange, so maybe we can agree on three thousand?'

'We're not the banks, we don't do big sums, so our profits are lower.'

'I don't need an economic breakdown of your small business, thank you. You're here ripping people off and you know your sob story is too much. Let's make this fair.'

They look at each other. 'How much have you got?'

'Three thousand dollars.'

'Where are you from?'

'Take a guess.'

'Oh, yeah! How is it in Australia?'

'It's shit. So? Can you do three thousand? That's still heaps profitable for you.'

'Two thousand eight hundred,' he says firmly.

'That's a rip-off.'

'I'm the only one in this *whole street* that can guarantee you genuine bills.'

I like these guys, kind of. It's hard not to at least see people as human when they're willing to take off their scarves and show me who they are. I know they want to trade with me. It's their business, after all. But at what rate will they draw the line? Where does their bluff stop?

'Don't be stupid,' one cautions. 'We know you need the money or you wouldn't be here right now.'

'Well, I'm not stupid enough to go for that shit rate you gave me. I'll just come back next week,' I add, and turn to go, praying to God's prophets my bluff works.

I'm almost at the taxi, striding, not looking back, when one of them yells, 'Stop!'

I turn around. They've followed me out here.

'Listen, I can tell you're desperate. But so are we, okay? No one comes here on a Friday wanting to exchange thousands of dollars. And I am merely doing what a good businessman does.'

'Taking advantage of the needy?'

'Precisely.'

I think for an impossible minute. I know I have no choice. I'm not just being stubborn here; I need a good exchange. I don't know if what I've got is enough for two tickets as it is.

I look them each in the eye, one to another, and make my final offer.

'Two thousand nine hundred.'

They glance at each other, then smile.

'Okay, two thousand nine hundred, you big-mouthed Australian. You're getting a good deal in this market.'

'As are you.'

'Where's your money?'

'Just to be clear. How can I be sure you're giving me real cash?'

'I will withdraw the cash for you from an ATM. Any bank *you* nominate. It will all be cash you can physically grab from the machine. I told you, we're the only legit ones here.'

I take a signature deep breath and accompany the two men to a nearby ATM. The driver collects my money from the boot and hangs back a little bit, to make sure the two men don't get up to no good; he doesn't have to do this, but I'm grateful he does.

The men hand me a wad of cash.

'All legit.'

I read the receipt closely. It's not adding up.

'This says it's only eight million. I should get close to nine million. You've even reneged on your original two thousand eight hundred.'

'Listen up,' says one of the men. 'Just be thankful here.' His friend nods. They both step very close to me.

'Be thankful you found someone who's honest enough not to swap your cash for fakes. Be thankful you didn't find someone who would've stabbed you anyway. Be thankful you get to live in a country like Australia while the young men here go rotting. I have a master's degree. A fucking master's in Economics and I'm here on a public holiday, risking jail just to exchange some money for pompous pricks like you. Eight million is good for you. I could have ripped you off, you know. But I can see you're just like me. I can tell you're struggling. But the comparisons stop there. Your struggle is not our struggle. So shake my hand, take your money, and just. Be. Thankful.'

He extends his hand. I take it. We shake. Then I nod and, without another word, I get back inside the cab.

❖ ❖ ❖

At 7 pm, I wait, stiff and sweating, outside the freight-shipping agency. Forty minutes later, it's still closed.

To offset my nerves, I call Moe Greene and Ali to make sure everything is good to go back home. I'm hoping they'll have stuffed it up somehow and I'll have to argue down the phone, but to my mixed delight and disappointment, they've performed perfectly. I thank and congratulate them. Back to my nervous sweats.

At 8 pm, a tall bearded man in a black shirt appears. His face is severe. I immediately connect him to the Basij—Iran's religious military arm.

'Are you the one who called me? Why aren't you wearing black? Didn't you say your father's passed away?'

Before I can respond, a mob of black-shirted Basijis pushes past us into the shop. I can't be seen by these people as 'morally loose' at all. They are wearing black to mark the anniversary of Imam Reza's death—the whole town is wearing black, and they don't even have dead fathers. By this stage, at least I have some decent facial growth, which might tip the scales back in my favour.

'I can get him on the plane,' the man says. 'It will cost you by the kilo.'

'He was 103 kilos,' I say. We'd weighed him at Reza's Paradise.

'Tall?'

'Just over six foot.'

'So a big box then. That'll get him close to 120 kilos all up.'

He bangs some numbers on the calculator. 'It's two thousand six hundred US.'

I breathe deep. That's more than a return ticket for a living person, one you have to keep cool with recycled air and serve in-flight drinks and food.

'Expensive, right?' he says. 'Freight always is. Besides, you can't just show up this late and expect something cheap.'

This piques my interest: so cheap is possible, at certain times, for certain people, certain things.

'I didn't have my exit papers till yesterday. I didn't time his death, you know.'

'That's the price.'

'You said bring Iranian currency.'

'No problems. We buy one US dollar for three thousand three hundred, so…8.5 million.'

I remember the dodgy black marketeer: eight million. *Just. Be. Thankful.*

'Brother,' I breathe. 'I already had a number done on me at the exchange today, three thousand Aussie dollars for eight million Iranian.'

'Yeah, it gets rough,' he nods sympathetically. 'So what do you want to do?'

I am not aware that I have many options left.

'Even if my family wires me money, it'll take a day or two at best.'

He thinks. 'Didn't you say your visa was expiring tomorrow?'

'Yes, that's the issue,' I say, a little testily. But I'm grateful to have found the one bureaucrat in Iran who doesn't apparently suffer from short-term memory problems. I'd explained about my visa this afternoon, and over the phone no less; I'd got used to my story vanishing, forever out of mind, the minute I left a person's eyeline.

'But then you must have had an exit ticket. A return flight.'

'It's to France.'

'Who was your carrier?'

'Emirates.'

'Hmm. And who did you fly in with?'

'Qatar.'

'Hmmmm. And your dad?'

'Yes, he was to go back on Qatar Airways to Australia.'

'Excellent!' he says. 'It's an easy solve, we have a good relationship with Qatar Air. I'll do this for you, I'll change your father's return leg into your name, so you can fly in his seat instead. We still have to send *him* as a shipment, of course…'

Against the odds, this man is so helpful, and so innovative too. The problem is, he's still a businessman, and I'm still half a million short. I have just enough scrap money for food and taxis to get me through tomorrow, but nowhere near enough to cover the shortfall—$150.

'I still have my Emirates ticket to France. What about that? It's worth five hundred dollars, and it's a flexi-flight. So they can refund me the money if I cancel it. I could just nominate your bank account. You'd have it in no time.'

'Hmm. What currency?'

We both know it's Australian. 'You'll have the money in your account,' I say. 'Isn't that what matters?'

'Are you some kind of wiseguy? I'd need to convert it to US. And I don't care how strong your dollar is, we *always* lose against that. Then, there's the interest on these fourteen days I'd have to put the money up, and—'

'Have it all!' I cry. 'Fuck it, just have it all! I'll give you my eight million now, then that whole five hundred dollars. That's three hundred dollars, a million, more than your asking price. Just get me out of here, and get my father home.'

He thinks about it for a moment. 'Okay, that works,' he shrugs.

I make the call to Emirates; they're accommodating as all get-out. As I do, the man places each and every bill under the scanner and subjects them to the blue-light test. Thumbs-up. The notes are good. They're all good.

They are *all* good.

They are all good.

I stand there, in a dream. Could it be that I will be out of here with Dad tomorrow?

I made it.

The man hands me my tickets. Or, my ticket. Dad's ticket in my name, and then a separate itinerary for my cargo.

'I will meet you in the airport tomorrow,' he says. 'Your flight is at 8.30 pm. Check-in closes at six-thirty. Don't be late.'

'I'll be there in the morning.'

'No, don't do that,' he says. 'The cemetery will transport the coffin directly to the freight terminal and, believe me, you don't want your dad out of cold storage for long.'

As I grab the tickets, it occurs to me that paper has a smell. Freedom is what it smells like. It looks like paper, but smells like freedom.

It is an algedonic moment. Bittersweet with a capital B. I spring up and out the door. I could fly, I am so light. Actually, screw the 'could'. I *will* fly. Tomorrow, I will.

STOLEN DREAMS
Melbourne, Australia, 2003

Dad's stroke of genius

When the planes hit the towers on 11 September 2001, things changed for our community. I must admit, with a name like Osamah, it would have been folly to think I'd get away without being searched 'extra randomly' at airports. However, I didn't bank on those extra checks seeping out into everyday life. At train stations. Shops. Even the local baker. These 'checks' weren't necessarily physical, but more psychological taunts and words similar to the ones I had heard as a young Arab boy in Iran. It was funny (in a totally not funny way) that here I was in Australia, where people were so advanced, yet 'go back, you desert monkey' and 'blow yourself up at home and leave me the virgins' were as common as the common Aussie fly. It seemed that no matter where you went on this planet, any global event could turn otherwise decent humans into creative phrase-makers slash mouth-frothing taunters.

More than ever, then, our community converged on the mosque—which suited my own conscience. Between Sisi and the

Amazing Medical Degree That Never Was, I liked being in a place where I got to be a good Muslim boy again.

Each night, Dad took our neighbours' social and religious questions after prayer. After September 11, these Q&A sessions could last a good three hours. I was there for all of them, approaching my tasks as the cleric's son with renewed levels of diligence.

It was past midnight, and we were all in need of some decent shut-eye, when a zealous Sayyed shouted: 'Your Excellency! Can you write a play about the Prophet's second war on the infidels? It will be a smash hit!'

Dad always wrote a play meant for performance in the mosque, which doubled as a makeshift theatre while the season ran its course. His scripts were populated mostly by the local husbands, and by yours truly, every year since 1995. What can I say? Bored Muslim mothers got obsessed with Aussie Rules. The dads turned into amateur thespians.

'Sayyed. I am going to write a different play this season. A musical.'

'About the Prophet's war! Please! It will be funny.'

'No.' Every year, another period piece; Dad had had enough. 'I'm going to write a contemporary show.'

A true director, he knew when to pause for effect.

'I'm going to write *Saddam: The Musical*.'

Sydney, Australia, November 2004

Playing Saddam

```
Curtains open.

We see: a lavish hall in Saddam's palace.
```

STOLEN DREAMS

A number of Saddam's elite bodyguards stand, unlit.

Also present (standing on designer sofas) are Saddam's henchmen: Chemical Ali, Izzat Ibrahim, Taha Yassin, Muhammad Al-Sahhaf and Saddam's son, Qusay.

Cue music: 'Stayin' Alive', by the Bee Gees.

Lights on Saddam Hussein, in uniform and beret, sporting his trademark moustache and aviators.

He stands in the middle of the hall, eerily charismatic. A Cuban cigar in hand.

The henchmen start to do their dance, also in full uniform.

Saddam, with stiff movements, belts out the opening number in his scratchy voice:

        SADDAM
Well, you can tell by the way I use my walk
I'm the nation's man, no time to talk.
The bombs are loud and America warm.
I've been kicked around since I was born.
And now it's alright, it's okay
The UN may look the other way.
We can try to understand
The New York attack's effect on man.
Whether you're a brother
Or whether you're a mother
You're stayin' alive, stayin' alive.
Feel Baghdad breakin'
And Iraq shakin'
And we're stayin' alive, stayin' alive.

        HENCHMEN
Ah, ha, ha, ha —
Stayin' alive.

Stayin' alive.
Ah, ha, ha, ha —
Stayin' aliiiiiiiiive.

    SADDAM
Well now, I get low and I get high
And if I can't get either I really try.
Got a block by the US on our booze
I'm a people's man and I just can't lose.
You know it's alright, it's okay.
I'll live to see another day.
We can try to understand
The New York attack's effect on man.
Whether you're a brother
Or whether you're a mother
You're stayin' alive, stayin' alive.
Feel our city breakin'
And my nation shakin'
And we're stayin' alive, stayin' alive.
Ah, ha, ha, ha —
Stayin' alive.
Stayin' alive.
Ah, ha, ha, ha —
Stayin' alive.

Life goin' nowhere.
Somebody help me.
Somebody help me, yeah.
Life goin' nowhere.
Somebody help me, yeah.

Except Iran
I don't want their help.
But Iraq's burning
Somebody help us.
Somebody help us, yeah.

```
        Get rid of the sanctions
        Bring back the friendship
        C'mon Bush
        Do it now!
        Stayin' alive
        Stayin' alive
        Stayin' aliiiiiiiiiiiiive.
```

The music stops, but the henchmen keep dancing.
Saddam looks at them with menace; they freeze.
Saddam laughs. They laugh. He laughs louder.
They laugh louder. He stops. One of them continues
laughing. He just signed his death contract.

❖ ❖ ❖

Saddam: The Musical was a roaring success.

After a sold-out season in Melbourne, we took it on the road—as far afield as Sydney, Shepparton and Cobram. Not all of this went smoothly. I had a shoe hurled at me in Shepparton. I guess you have to expect a mixed response when you're playing Saddam Hussein. In that scene, I was dancing over the corpse of a beloved Iraqi Sayyed.

In the end, more than 3000 Arabic speakers came out to see the show.

Dad was chuffed. Who wouldn't be? Two-time escapee, noted cleric—and now regular off-Broadway wunderkind, discovered late in life. There was an honest-to-God media frenzy in the Arabic papers—the first time in forever I'd had to polish my formal Arabic.

We were all chuffed, our little drama troupe from Fawkner-by-way-of-humanitarian-visa. Of course, we started to set our sights on bigger theatres, brighter lights.

San Francisco, USA, 6 August 2005

Osamah vs Hernandez

It's possible that the world was not quite ready for us.

The plan was to dispatch me to the Middle East to meet with the local theatre companies. Kuwait, the United Arab Emirates, Bahrain and Oman: Saddam's tyranny had reached all these lands over the decades, so we figured each would have a hungry, built-in audience. Best of all, we'd be playing to the masses, giving them some much-needed release from real historical atrocities. Nothing really lets you know that the past is over like watching Saddam Hussein dancing to a Bee Gees song.

But we got stalled on Kuwait. I spent three months there, cajoling Kuwaitis to accept our company. The Ministry of Information's censorship board kept us waiting for six months, before rejecting the play on undisclosed grounds.

No matter. The world was bigger than the Middle East—and the Middle East was all over the world. We were living proof of that. Detroit had a large Iraqi expat population, and through discussion with a number of local artists there, we managed to book a season at a large community centre. It wasn't Broadway, but it was closer than Shepparton, at least.

Soon enough, eight of us were touching down in San Francisco, with full hearts and crushed costumes crammed into our luggage. America: the land of the free.

◆ ◆ ◆

When Hernandez the Homeland Security officer led me into the interrogation room, he assured me this was all standard procedure.

Twelve hours in a drab room flooded by fluorescent light is a long standard procedure, if you ask me.

I was exhausted, jetlagged and starving—one pack of noodles this whole time.

Hernandez the Homeland Security Officer got to leave the room; I didn't. Now, he wandered back in and sat opposite me.

> HERNANDEZ
> One more time. What is the purpose of your visit to the United States?
>
> OSAMAH
> *(boldly)*
> I'm here to do a musical.
>
> HERNANDEZ
> You, OSAMAH, are doing a musical, about Saddam. Is that what I'm hearing?
>
> OSAMAH
> How many times do I have to tell you?
>
> HERNANDEZ
> *(nonchalant)*
> So tell me again. I like your accent.
>
> OSAMAH
> Christ, mate.
>
> HERNANDEZ
> Don't blaspheme.
>
> OSAMAH
> Muslims believe in Jesus too.
>
> HERNANDEZ
> You're not doing yourself or your friends out there any favours by being a smartass.

OSAMAH

Do you want me to say Muhammad instead of Jesus? Okay. Muhammad, Muhammad! Doesn't have the same ring to it. We have a show to do.

HERNANDEZ

So you say.

OSAMAH

So I know.

HERNANDEZ

And you rehearsed this play at a mosque.

OSAMAH

How many times do I have to repeat it? Yes. Yes. Yes.

HERNANDEZ

At a mosque? You want me to believe you were rehearsing a musical at a mosque? And the author of this play is what—a shake?

OSAMAH

He's a sheikh, not a banana smoothie. What is your problem, mate?

HERNANDEZ

I want to make sure you're here for the reasons you're saying you are.

OSAMAH

I told you, me, Mohammad, Mustafa, Ali, Hassan, Hussain, Jaber and Mahmoud are here to do a musical.

(OSAMAH and HERNANDEZ look at each other across the table. They are both thinking the exact same thing about what all those strange names sound like.)

OSAMAH
Goddammit, man. I mean, Muhammad-dammit, man. We're here to do a funny show. Want a ticket? You'd love it.

HERNANDEZ
We tend not to laugh at terrorism here.

OSAMAH
Oh, lighten up. The play is anti-terrorism.

HERNANDEZ
We'll see about that. The play is being translated as we speak. We *will* decipher this.

OSAMAH
Decipher this? Like it's in code?

(HERNANDEZ looks at him: you tell me.)

OSAMAH
We're all about peace, you know. There are over one billion of us in the world.

HERNANDEZ
More than three times the population of the States.

OSAMAH
What does that have to do with anything?
(pause)

Oh, I know what you're doing! Trying to get me to incriminate myself.

HERNANDEZ
(reasonably)
But you could take us down. It's simple math. Right?

OSAMAH
Wait, what? I mean, yes, we outnumber you but—hey! Don't type that! What did you type there?

(OSAMAH leans across the table to scrutinise the computer. HERNANDEZ swivels the screen away.)

OSAMAH
Just because my name's OSAMAH doesn't make me a terrorist. It might make me a dick, a prick, a fish stick, but not a terrorist. OSAMAH's actually a popular name. It means lion. There's a fun fact for ya: OSAMAH equals lion.

HERNANDEZ
We are writing everything down, OSAMAH. You better pick your words wisely.

OSAMAH
You better pick your words wisely. I'm an Australian citizen.

HERNANDEZ
The London Bombers were British, weren't they?

(OSAMAH throws up his hands. What can he say?)

HERNANDEZ
(grinning amicably)
Silence is a sign of defeat.

OSAMAH
Yeah, good on ya. We're gonna miss our connecting flight to Detroit —

HERNANDEZ
Believe me, that's the last of your worries.

(There's a large map of the United States on the wall. OSAMAH glances at it idly.)

STOLEN DREAMS

          HERNANDEZ
Why are you looking at the map?

          OSAMAH
I felt like it. You've never done something you felt like? Ever itch your balls under your desk at work? I. Felt. Like. It.

          HERNANDEZ
You have a lot of anger, OSAMAH. How would you feel if we bombed your country?

          OSAMAH
You planning to bomb Australia?

          HERNANDEZ
Don't be a wise-ass. I meant Iran.

          OSAMAH
Australia's my country, and unless you're planning to attack it I have nothing to say to you.

          HERNANDEZ
I meant I-*ran*. What is your connection to I-*ran*, OSAMAH?

          OSAMAH
I used to milk goats there. That's my connection.
      (seeing Hernandez is typing this)
Don't type the goats bit, can't you tell my tone?
      (a deep, frustrated breath)
I was born there.

          HERNANDEZ
      (dead serious)
So you didn't milk goats?

(OSAMAH just stares.)

          HERNANDEZ

What is your connection to I-rak?

          OSAMAH

My parents were born there. Why are you asking questions you already know the answers to? Modern-day technology not reached you yet?

          HERNANDEZ

You seem to know a lot about modern-day technology. A lot for an actor, no?

          OSAMAH
          (insulted on behalf of his fellow actors)

I can build a computer from the ground up.

          HERNANDEZ

Yeah?

          OSAMAH

That's hard for you to believe too? Muslims can 'do' things.

          HERNANDEZ

Oh, I know what Muslims can do. Do you know how to hack into a computer, OSAMAH?

          OSAMAH

What a dumb question, no offence. If I was a hacker you think I'd just get on my knees and tell you?
          (realising)
That might have come out wrong.

(HERNANDEZ raises his eyebrows, leaves the room. Time passes. He comes back with a folder.)

HERNANDEZ
We've made some calls back to Australia. Your police aren't too happy with you.

OSAMAH
I got some unpaid fines.

HERNANDEZ
Some?

OSAMAH
Okay, ten, fifteen thousand dollars' worth.

HERNANDEZ
You're a real lawbreaker, aren't you?

OSAMAH
I was a dick as a driver. Always driving without my P-plates displayed, driving unregistered cars, couldn't afford it. So the fines kept piling up. That doesn't make me a terrorist.

HERNANDEZ
But you're angry with the system.

OSAMAH
I'm angry with myself.

HERNANDEZ
If I were someone like you, OSAMAH, I'd be angry with myself too. You have a history of lying.

OSAMAH
When you're young, you can't think. We've all told lies, haven't we?

HERNANDEZ
Not about a whole college degree.

OSAMAH
There was a lot of community pressure.

HERNANDEZ
You even said it yourself, 'OSAMAH' means lyin'.

OSAMAH
(pause)
Lion. Not lying...Why would anyone's name mean 'lying'?

HERNANDEZ
OSAMAH. OSAMAH. OSAMAH. Don't suppose you know where the other OSAMA is?

(HERNANDEZ laughs at his own joke.)

OSAMAH
I thought you didn't find terrorism funny.

(Enter stage left a tall, white man. He is the HUMAN LIE DETECTOR.)

HERNANDEZ
Well, now you're in trouble.

HUMAN LIE DETECTOR
Are you comfortable there, sir?

OSAMAH
Five-star luxury.

HUMAN LIE DETECTOR
You guys seem far too organised to be a theatre company.

(OSAMAH is again insulted on behalf of all artists.)

HUMAN LIE DETECTOR
The game is over, OSAMAH. Who are the whores?

OSAMAH
I'm sorry, who are the whats?

HUMAN LIE DETECTOR
Name the whores. We translated the script.
There's mention of whores —

(OSAMAH bursts out laughing. There is a scene in the musical in which Saddam's whores come to console their president; all these roles are played by men, comically dressed as harlots.)

OSAMAH
Yeah man, I'll name the whores: Mustafa, Mohammed and Mahmoud. You won't find tramps like those three.

C'mon, mate, what do you want from us? We're low on resources. People have to play multiple roles.

HUMAN LIE DETECTOR
Your mosque's resources seem to be pretty darn good.

OSAMAH
We rehearsed at the mosque because we *didn't* have resources — we couldn't afford anywhere else. Plus Dad okayed it.

HUMAN LIE DETECTOR
The sheikh. Of course he okayed it.
> (*His tone changes to a game attempt at sympathy.*)

You had nothing to do with it. We're not blaming you. We just want to know who planned it. You say your father was the one who wrote this?

OSAMAH
Yes.

HUMAN LIE DETECTOR
So he's the architect behind this. Tell me what the whores stand for. Are they some kind of code?

OSAMAH
You're like a cartoon character, fair dinkum.

HERNANDEZ
That's just Aussie lingo, sir.

(The HUMAN LIE DETECTOR stares daggers at HERNANDEZ.)

HUMAN LIE DETECTOR
And you'll be in the country a handful of days. That's kind of a quick trip, wouldn't you say?

OSAMAH
We are here to do three shows, and then we go back. If it's a success, we might come back later. Hey, I just realised — that means the three of us might get to hang out again!

HUMAN LIE DETECTOR
Very efficient responses, OSAMAH. Can you name five New York landmarks?

OSAMAH
Anyone can.

(HERNANDEZ and the HUMAN LIE DETECTOR are at the edge of their seats.)

OSAMAH
Times Square. Statue of Liberty. Central Park. The Towers.

STOLEN DREAMS

> HUMAN LIE DETECTOR
> Ground Zero, OSAMAH.

> OSAMAH
> Ground Zero...David Letterman.

> HUMAN LIE DETECTOR
> That was rather fast.

> OSAMAH
> Shall I do it slurred?

> HUMAN LIE DETECTOR
> I'll be sure to pass on your regards to Mr Letterman. He'll be thrilled to have a Muslim fan.

(The HUMAN LIE DETECTOR takes a long, meaningful pause. HERNANDEZ pants with anticipation.)

> HUMAN LIE DETECTOR
> You know, the thing is you claimed even if you *were* a terrorist, you wouldn't admit to it, so we're in a bit of a knot here.

> OSAMAH
> I said if I was a hacker I wouldn't admit it and it came out wrong. Please. I stink. I haven't had food, I've been here for fourteen hours.

> HUMAN LIE DETECTOR
> Name the bombers, OSAMAH.

> OSAMAH
> What bombers? What are you trying to pin on me?

> HUMAN LIE DETECTOR
>   *(holds up OSAMAH's mobile phone)*
> Is this your phone?

OSAMAH
Shit. What have you planted on my phone?

HUMAN LIE DETECTOR
Nothing planted. Just your own messages:

'Let's watch them get killed from front-row seats.'

'I want our boys to destroy them.'

'They will eat our dust.'

Are these not yours?

(OSAMAH looks at the messages of 'terror' and they *are* his messages. Then, it all registers. He begins to laugh uncontrollably.)

OSAMAH
Yes! I am a proud Bomber! And yes, those are my messages!

(The HUMAN LIE DETECTOR and HERNANDEZ look at OSAMAH, surprised but victorious.)

OSAMAH
I'll name the Bombers: Kevin Sheedy, he's the top dig, James Hird and Matthew Lloyd, they're definitely hardcore Bombers.

HUMAN LIE DETECTOR
(after a long pause)
Wow. One's gotta admire your tenacity. You sell out to a thousand zealots. Rehearse every answer. Hide your sicko messages behind a football team and come to this country prepared.

OSAMAH
What do you mean?

>   HUMAN LIE DETECTOR
> It means you won't be dining with your
> seventy-two virgins on our soil. We're
> deporting you out.
>
>   OSAMAH
>   *(desperately)*
> I'll sing you a song from the play...
>
> (OSAMAH begins to belt out 'Stayin' Alive',
> complete with the scratchy voice of Saddam.
>
> The HUMAN LIE DETECTOR throws up his hands in
> disgust.)
>
>   HUMAN LIE DETECTOR
> Deported!
>
>   OSAMAH
>   *(hysterical)*
> No! God has cleared a path for me! I must enter
> the country and carry this out! It's God's plan!
>
>   *(realising this all sounds pretty
>   terrible)*
> Should I sing you the closing number?

❖ ❖ ❖

I was thereby deemed unfit to enter the United States, and was removed, effective immediately. It turned out we also had the wrong visas, so it wasn't all Starsky and Hutch's fault. The problem was, we'd been expelled for a period of seven years, so even if we were to leave and gain proper documents, they'd never have let us back in.

It was possible, I realised, that our theatre troupe had been dealt a bum hand from the start. Nobody had ever mentioned anything about our visas before—if someone had happened to not want to deal with us, they sure would've made a convenient loophole.

The rest of the troupe, I could already tell, were all having the same thought. We just *knew* what had happened, without saying a word. That's how close you get in the theatre.

They clapped us in cuffs and dragged us aboard a flight home before the first-class passengers could board. I looked at them, waiting in the terminal: each and every one of them frightened. All they saw was a line of dishevelled Muslim men being tugged around by Homeland Security officers. I wondered if any of them would flip out and try to get on another flight.

'Make yourselves comfortable,' the air marshals suggested, and took off our handcuffs once we were safely tucked at the rear of the plane, away from the white people. We chattered in Arabic all through the long flight, in our best attempt to piss them off, but they were actually pretty nice guys.

The truth is, I was wrecked by the ordeal, and all the nice guys in the world couldn't have helped that. Iran and Iraq were in the business of stealing your dreams; now the US was as well? I knew we'd get new dreams, new ideas, new musicals—our theatre troupe would rise again. But I also got the feeling our options were narrowing, in this big, little world we called home.

CLEARANCE

Mashhad, Iran, 2013: zero days until visa expires

I spend the night walking around the sleepless city, amid the pilgrims—surging millions, all here to pay tribute to someone they, too, lost long ago.

It is a sea of people, and none of them are mine. I wish my darling soulmate were here. I wish my daughter was, too. Soft snow falls on my grey jacket and slides right off again.

Dawn breaks, and there's nothing for it but to cab it to Reza's Paradise.

I arrange with the main office to release Dad and have him taken to the airport. The ambulance driver is the same one who brought Dad's body here, days prior. He does not remember me, but I remember him very well.

When he learns I want the airport, he gets it. 'Wow, are you *still* in Iran?'

◆ ◆ ◆

I arrive at two-thirty—way early, but I need everything to go smoothly from this point on.

Dad's body is placed on a gharry. The ambulance goes.

I clutch my ticket and my exit papers, waiting for the other shoe to drop.

❖ ❖ ❖

I walk into the small office in the middle of freightland. Outside the office, there are forklifts and aircrafts and their commotions, their personnel. Inside the office is a tranquil, quiet zone.

'*Salam*,' I greet the clerk. He, of course, sips tea.

'What carrier are you after?'

'Qatar.'

'Aircraft's not even here. You're too early. Sit, sit down. Do you want some tea?'

'No, thank you. But if you could just take care of this?' The main airport terminal—where I have to check in our other cargo, namely me—is six kilometres from here. About an hour's walk. And even without my father, I am going to have a lot of luggage to drag over.

'Sit down. Relax. You look stressed,' he advises. 'Would you like some tea?'

'No, I wouldn't.'

'Are you sure?'

'I'm really, really sure.'

He grins. 'You are not doing *taarof*?'

'When is the Keyhan guy coming? He said he'd meet me here.'

'He won't be coming today, but don't worry. We'll see you load the box in safely. May I see your exit papers? And are you sure you don't want tea?'

I hand him all my paperwork. He calls Qatar Air. He murmurs for ten minutes. I wait impatiently, eyes closed.

He hangs up and snaps me out of it. 'No,' he says simply. 'Qatar says they don't have clearance.'

'*Clearance?*' I say. My life flashes before my eyes—or at least what my life's become: this one job, these million jobs, every paper under the sun, every department.

'They don't have Australian clearance. Melbourne Airport doesn't have the paperwork.'

'That's impossible,' I whisper.

'Sorry,' he says. 'Tea?'

When I spoke with my brothers, they said they'd organised it days ago.

'Your sorry doesn't do,' I say, tight and firm. 'This is impossible.'

He calls the airline again. My watch reads two-fifty. I watch him while he's speaking. His air of regret doesn't change.

He hangs up. 'Sorry,' he says again. 'They have no record of such a shipment, and apparently your country has tough laws on human remains. That was the Qatar Airways head office in Tehran I just spoke with. They cannot authorise this boarding until Australia gives the green light.'

'Australia will accept his body.'

His eyebrows lift beatifically: maybe they will, maybe they won't.

A horrid thought occurs to me.

'What will happen to my dad?'

'You'll have to take him back to the morgue,' he says. 'You can't leave him out there, of course.'

Surely there is someone who can make it all okay—who can press the okay button. Who can green-light this event.

Someone who is human, and who understands everything.

In lieu of such a person, I could at least call my bro.

'May I use your phone?' I ask.

The man sips his tea. 'Don't you have a phone?'

'Mine only works with wi-fi.'

He looks at me sadly. 'There's wi-fi in the main terminal,' he says.

❖ ❖ ❖

I leave my luggage and take the six kilometres at the fiercest run.

I draw energy from the universe, import it from the past: every jog I've ever taken, every lap round every pool. I will my body to keep going. It just can't stop now.

I throw myself through the doors with one hand and with the other, switch the wi-fi on.

Voila.

I open Viber and get Moe Greene on the phone.

'But I did it,' he says, baffled. 'They never sent a confirmation email. *Oh.*'

I can hear Mum and my younger siblings sobbing in the room. He must have me on speakerphone. I try to calm them down. 'It'll be okay,' I say. 'If God exists, He is watching.'

I ask Moe to get in touch with the Aussies and let them know to expect a call from Qatar Airways Iran. 'When?' he asks.

I feel ill. 'Just as soon as I can sprint back to the freight terminal, bro.'

And so I bolt back. Twenty minutes later, I am there, in the tranquil office in the middle of freightland. I fall through the door, ready to pass out.

'Wow, that was quick,' the man says, impressed.

'I called my brother,' I pant, 'and we have 100 per cent confirmation. *One hundred per cent.* You can call Australia and find out for yourself.'

He sighs. 'Believe me, son, I want to put your father on the plane. I really do. But I don't want to lose my job. Put yourself in my shoes.'

'Great,' I say. 'I forgive you. Can you please call Qatar?' It's already 4 pm. I still have to check in myself.

'Okay,' he says. 'Would you like some tea?'

I wonder if he is messing with me. I don't think so.

'No, no tea for me. Just boarding the plane, please.'

He speaks to Qatar headquarters in Tehran again, sipping on tea with one hand, sugar cubes in the other, the phone wedged precariously between his chin and shoulder.

They place him on hold while they contact Australia. I sit there silently. Three minutes tick by on the wall clock. Each tick jolts my heart.

Finally, he hangs up. 'No,' he whispers. 'Qatar's been calling Australia, but no one is picking up. It's 11 pm on a Saturday there. Apparently that's the worst time.'

'Who are they calling?'

'They tried the manager of Qatar in Melbourne. All the offices are shut.'

'Please, get them to try the airport. The freight terminal. Anyone.'

He nods. He's a sweet man.

Twelve minutes pass, fast and slow.

I can tell from this sweet man's face that nothing's going to change.

He hangs up the phone. 'The men in the warehouse say their supervisor needs to give the okay. They have no knowledge of the shipment themselves.'

'So let them call the supervisor.'

'They refused. They said it's too late to wake up the boss.'

'It's Saturday night. He'll be out. That's what they do in Australia. Tell them to call him, please. He will have a mobile phone.'

But the sweet man's hands are going nowhere near the phone.

'I think you should get your father's remains back in the fridge,' he says. 'And leave Iran tonight for Qatar with your ticket. From Qatar, you get a ticket back to Tehran and on re-entry, explain your circumstances to the officials. They'll issue a temporary visa. We can sort this out next week.'

I consider this. It sounds reasonable. But it also sounds so wrong.

'I'm not putting him back in a fridge,' I say. 'He's been in a fridge all week. We want to bury him. My family. The community. Everyone wants him back. And I just can't keep doing this. Surely someone can say yes.'

'Unless there's written proof, we cannot authorise this boarding.'

'I will get you that proof,' I growl.

✦ ✦ ✦

By 4.37 pm, I am back in the main terminal. I've got the wi-fi switched on, and I'm gasping down the phone to Moe.

'I don't *have* the confirmation email,' he says. 'That's the whole problem.'

'Do you have any correspondence?'

'Let me see…okay, yes. There was an initial email. But that's not the same thing, Osamah.'

'It doesn't have to be.'

And that's when I tell Moe that I am going to write the confirmation email myself. All I need is an email address, letterhead and signature; I'll fill in the body myself, and send it to Qatar.

Unfortunately, the initial email is just an automated response, no letterhead or signature—a few lines of text is all. 'It does have the right email address,' Moe says.

'That's all I need, bro!' I shout.

This is not new territory. Moe and I have spent our whole lives coming up against the authorities and finding creative workarounds. All week, I've felt so helpless—so many procedures and forms. But a bit of deviant behaviour in the hope of doing some good? This is my forte.

I find an internet kiosk tucked away behind a hamburger joint. A young man is on it. I approach, keeping my cool. With the adrenaline pumping through me, it's hard not to jump him.

'Excuse me, how long do you think you're going to be?' I ask.

'I don't know. Twenty minutes?' he replies, not looking up at me.

I clear my throat. 'I will give you ten thousand tomans if you get off right now.'

Now he looks up at me.

'But it's just three thousand *an hour* to use.'

'Come on! I need it urgently.' I wave the large note—my last dime—at him.

And he takes it, still processing what it means. The time on the monitor reads 4.45 pm. I have work to do.

❖ ❖ ❖

At 5.18 pm I burst back into the tiny office in freightland.

'I have forwarded,' I pant, 'the email, from Australia, to your office.'

'Sit down, sit down,' the man urges. 'Would you like some water?'

This completely throws me. 'No tea?' I want to ask. Instead, I say, 'Yes, but not now. Just check the email first please.'

My forgery is simple, though it has an elaborate trail. I think it looks pretty clean, considering the speed.

And all it needs to do is look clean, if I'm lucky. It does say *we accept the body*—but in English, which the man can't read. So he simply drinks more tea. He nods at me, approvingly. He calls up Tehran again.

He stays on the line, downing mug after mug of tea, for an alarming thirty minutes. Not once today have I seen this man get up to pee. More alarming still: Qatar Airways is verifying the email. Because the Australian warehouse knows nothing of the body, they need to make an 'executive decision'.

He hangs up. He sets down his tea. 'I'm afraid the email won't do,' he whispers.

'You said if I *gave* you the confirmation…'

'Yes,' he agrees. 'But I am just an employee. This goes back to the airline. They said the email needed to have been sent to *them*, is the thing. Why was it sent to your brother and not the Qatar office, they asked.'

So here we are. It was a good forgery. It was not enough.

It is 5.47 pm on the wall, I idly notice. The flight is all but closed. And the answer is no.

I remember everyone I have encountered, right from Aioli Cop to the countless tea-sippers to the knife-wielders on the bus to the man punching me outside the airline agency to the homeless woman to the drivers to the father-to-be soldier and the deputy to the black-market exchange boys. It all seems years ago.

Something tells me that I need to capture this moment. It is the moment when all my efforts have finally come to naught.

So I hold up my phone, find some good light, and take a selfie. I frame Dad's coffin behind my shoulders and face. He lies in a box, on a trolley. The shutter clicks.

I look scarier than the coffin. I have deteriorated by the day.

❖ ❖ ❖

At 6.03 pm, the phone rings in the tea-sipping man's office. Three minutes into the call, I notice that he's begun to speak with more energy. I can't help but sit up and lean closer to the desk. His mug of tea is empty by the time he's put on hold, but instead of filling it, he chooses to update me.

'A manager up the food chain heard your story from a colleague,' he says. 'And now he's personally trying to get this whole thing sorted. He's been on the phone with Qatar headquarters, in Qatar. He's the only man in Tehran who has the power to call them. You're a lucky man, Osamah. Inshallah you're sorted… oh, hang on.'

They've taken him off hold.

He listens without responding. I read his face for clues, but it's blank. I pray with every fibre, to everyone I can. *Please, Imam Reza. Please, God. Please, Universe. Please. Please. Please.*

The man hangs up the phone.

'You can go. They said yes. You can go.'

My body floods with chilly goosebumps.

'Huh?' I say.

'Qatar in Qatar have said yes. They've said yes. You can go.'

'I can go?' I ask him.

'Your father must have been a special man. This is just plain miraculous.'

As for me, I just plain can't take it anymore. The whole week catches up with me in one explosive surge. I collapse on the office floor, and that's when I realise: my dad is dead, and I will never see him again in my life. I'll never see his smile again, we'll never talk about anything, we'll never eat felafels again, I'll never hold his hands like a kid. And so I bawl my eyes out, for the first time since he died. I half get up, crouching—almost supplicating. I weep and howl and claw the carpet.

And then I hear the sweet man, shouting over my sobbing.

'Are you going to cry or catch your plane? Check-in closes in twenty minutes. Forget about your luggage. I'll send it on a forklift.'

My mouth doesn't know what to do: keep crying. Smile. Fall apart. 'Thank you, sir,' I finally stutter.

'Don't thank me. Just run.'

I look at Dad's coffin, one last time. The grey-pink sky above. I do say, 'Thank you,' for good measure. And then it's time to go.

REPENTANCE

Melbourne, Australia, 2002

The plot unravels

The day my first, false year at university ended, I floated around on cloud nine. All around me, on campus, students were celebrating the end of exams and assignments. I had no such hurdles, but somehow that made it all the sweeter—I'd studied all year, just as hard as them, maybe, and I hadn't even *had* to. No professor was grading me; I was wasting no fees. I was a self-made man, my own teacher. I thought I was ready to sit a placement test and get into my Science degree. I felt no guilt at all about sharing the elation of everybody around me.

I ran inside the house, exhausted and happy—the wake of a hard-won achievement. Immediately, though, I sensed the mood of the room was dark and electric.

My whole family was sitting in the lounge room, ashen. It looked like an intervention.

Dad held up two papers.

'In one hand I have this,' he said sombrely. 'A paper you showed us, claiming you got 99.9. In my other hand, however, there's this paper, where the figure is 68.7. So, Osamah, I'll ask once and once only. Which score is the real one?'

Slam. The world collapsed around me.

My chest got tight like a rope looped around it and knotted, tighter and tighter. The rope looped again, knotting and knotting, larger and heavier and more choking. Then my heart got pressed under a shipping container filled with tons of raw metal. Then somebody threw me thousands of feet underwater and my lungs filled up. I dropped to the floor, sobbing.

As I went down, Dad stood up and towered over me.

'What were you thinking—that you'd become a pretend doctor and treat pretend patients?'

'I'm sorry, Dad. I'm so sorry,' I managed to finally breathe.

'Save your apology for the others,' he responded, and walked out of the room, leaving me bawling.

Repercussions

By 'others', my father did not just mean my family. He meant all the others. Everybody.

Dad walked ahead of me into the mosque, grimly. I trailed, wan and sorrowful.

At the door stood Luay, handing out photocopies of my true results to the gathering crowd.

I looked up from the ground and caught a glimpse of my future bride, Yomna. I had thought my disgrace may have had one silver lining—that her family would call off the engagement. Unfortunately, my future in-laws had been disappointingly supportive. Her father had just said, 'We all make mistakes.' I could atone, lucky for me, through marrying his daughter—a chance to prove myself an honest man.

Yomna gave me a supportive thumbs-up. I returned a sickly smile and stood before the congregation. Literally one thousand eyes on me.

'The Prophet has said,' I began, '"Lying is a sin which burns away the soul as fire burns through wood."'

Deep breaths.

'Hence I stand before you all and before God, offering my repentance, and inshallah with enough of my soul left unburned that it can all heal again. Not because I was caught, but because I allowed myself to drag this thing out for so long. Alas, I have failed before you and God.'

I felt there should be more, but I came up with nothing. 'Thank you,' I said weakly, and stepped down from the lectern.

Sayyed Ghaffar seized the microphone in a caricature of grimness, barely disguising his giddy delight.

'We've now heard it,' he burbled glumly. 'Where to now? I hear everyone ask. Our beloved sheikh has done a reasonable job raising his children. But…'

He looked regretful.

'If it weren't for my son Luay's vigilance, who knows how far Osamah would have taken this? I do not see the need for the sheikh to step down—not immediately. Noah, the Prophet of God, couldn't tame his own infidel son. Was the Prophet at fault when his son was no good? Of course he wasn't. But if this were Luay, I know in my heart I could not live with the shame. I know in my heart I could never continue as a role model for my people.'

What was there to say? Dad excused himself from the hall. In his absence, deathly silence invaded. Nobody knew what to do, including Sayyed Ghaffar. He stepped down from the lectern, and we all trickled away.

When I got home: an email from Sisi.

Hi Osamah,
I heard about your degree. I was saddened for you.

I was also saddened that you didn't tell me. I wouldn't have judged you.

It's been painful to hear from community members. Your news has been all over these days. Every house we visit, people are saying: oh, did you hear what the cleric's son did?

They're also saying you're engaged to someone else. I couldn't believe that at first either.

I wish you could be here and see how hard it is to write this without crying.

I am writing this packing my suitcase to go to the airport and meet my husband. That's right. My parents found out we were together. There's only so long you can keep that kind of secret. So there is this guy I am now engaged to. He seems okay.

I can't believe it has spiralled out of control like this, but it has. Our temporary marriage was expiring anyway, and I'm not sure what the divorce procedure is but I'm going to ask you to do that, please.

I wish you and your wife a happy life. You are really Da Kool Guy and you deserve everything good that comes your way.

Sisi

Airport run

I didn't even get dressed. I sped to the airport in my trackpants.

I wandered through the international terminal, lost in the surges of strangers. Hundreds of people, none of them her, all trying to get somewhere important.

Then, there she was—surrounded by family. How could I get her attention? I wanted to rush over, grab her and run. But that was impossible. All I could do was stand vaguely in her sightline and hope for the best.

She spotted me across the airport. I could see her eyes widen and her legs tighten.

I rubbed my forehead with my index finger, pointing subtly towards the bathrooms. Then I unlocked my eyes from hers, fully aware I might never see her again.

When I got to the bathrooms, I hunted through the ever-changing crowd to find her again, but nothing. Finally I spotted her family, but where was Sisi? It was hard to get a good look.

I turned around. Bang. There she was. She punched me hard on the chest.

I grabbed her hand and hugged her, not saying a word.

I wished we could do this forever, but we both knew time was running out. I took a letter out of my pocket and shoved it in her hand. And then, before I could do something smarter, or stupider, I let go and hurried away.

Beautiful Sisi,
I have no words. But I am sorry.

Everything I did, I did because I was afraid I would lose you.

Well, in the end, I did lose you, and I have nothing but regret.

I can promise you on the souls of all those martyred in the war that I did not touch Yomna. I was working on a plan to escape this marriage and was buying myself time.

Community and family pressure made this incredibly tough (I can't think of a stronger word). I'm still not sure how I could have done this better if I had the chance all over again. It is so raw.

I'm sorry I dragged you into this. I have nothing else. I am just sorry.

Wedding day

I cannot remember the physical details of the march up the aisle towards Yomna. With each step through the mosque, my mind went back a hundred, until I'd gone back to before I was born. This is called having your life flash before your eyes, and I knew it was not traditionally something that happened unless you were dying.

Before I knew it, though, I was reading the vows and exchanging the rings with Yomna. I sat on the chair, alone in a tux, before close to a thousand segregated onlookers. Yomna had been wheeled back to the women's section by the time I realised I was married.

People read the *Fatiha* for us; some even smiled. I had made my atonement, and had been forgiven. I had been married. I was a man.

People lined up to offer their congratulations. Abu Ghazi, the mosque's resident octogenarian, kissed my cheeks three times and used the distraction to slip a pill into my hand.

'One hour before bed,' he whispered through the gaps in his teeth. 'The rocket will launch and keep launching.'

After Abu Ghazi was one of the white friends I'd made in the library. 'Big fuckin' turnout!' he exclaimed. 'Shit, I'm not meant to swear in a mosque.'

'No.'

'But your mob don't speak English, do they?'

All around him was evidence to the contrary: mosque members, openly glaring.

'Holy fuck,' he whispered. 'So no alcohol, right?'

'No,' I replied, deep in my own thoughts.

'So it's just beer? How do you guys do it? Anyway, should go say hi to your old man. What do I call him? Your Holiness?'

And then there was dancing. Freestyle Arab—think hip-hop but clumsier. And then the cars honking, and Yomna and I were shoved into the limo.

Moe Greene was our driver. He smiled over his shoulder. 'Not bad, bro. Beautiful bride. Sick car. You done well. Congrats!'

Our eyes met for a second, and we used that second to say more than we could possibly vocalise.

The car crawled out of the courtyard, inching us towards our new home. Yomna's father had found us a place directly behind his own; he'd taken care of our bond and our first month's rent as a bonus. I'd maxed out my credit card filling this home with the necessary appliances. My tux was stuffed with cash from guests at the wedding, but we still couldn't afford a real honeymoon.

I kept forgetting Yomna was in the car. I noticed she was grabbing my hand, and idly realised this was the first time we'd touched each other. Each red light only delayed the inevitable; I was about to have sex with a stranger. I prayed for the lights to last longer, but they never lasted long enough.

I dug into my jacket pocket, down past the money, and found Sisi's email I had printed out. I clutched it. Where was she? What if she was getting married right now? We could share the gold medal for Synchronised Arranged Weddings at the Muslim Olympics. I let loose the tattered laugh of a madman, causing my wife to let go of my hand and Moe Greene to glance over his shoulder.

Three dozen hoon-mobiles tailed us to the house, horns honking, music blaring. I'd seen the cops often enough at just the wrong moment that I prayed they'd show up right now.

Where are you, policemen? Come arrest all these law-breaking Muslims. They've all got their heads stuck out the window and they're not wearing seatbelts, for God's sake! Moe Greene was actually unlicensed, and had an abiding, much-publicised love for the smell of burning rubber on a rental. I couldn't call the cops myself—he was my little bro—but I *could* pray for some racist Aussie to report the bunch of rowdy Moozlemz on the road.

No racist Aussie came.

We were rapidly closing on our happy new home, but everything was slowing down. The theory of general relativity had vexed me in high school, but everything finally clicked. With every second, I felt my skin cells aging. The world muted, save for a dark, constant droning—the same one you hear late at night when a TV channel is no longer broadcasting.

My head filled with strobe lights, popping and flashing. I asked Moe to pull over at the 7-Eleven, a strange one where I didn't know any of the employees.

'Bottle of water,' I croaked. Moe Greene imperceptibly nodded.

He found one, and pulled over. The long train of community members was doing its best to pull over too.

I opened the door, gulped the fresh air, looked at the cars and looked back at Yomna.

The oxygen hit me, exploding through my lungs. It was a starlit, hot December.

I jumped out of the car, but held the door open.

'Yomna,' I said.

Yomna looked worried.

'I'm sorry for everything,' I said.

I closed the door and a strong spell was broken.

I sucked in another deep breath and took off running.

Hiding out

Summer was over, and I was still living in a shabby one-bedroom in Brunswick.

At the 7-Eleven on my wedding day, I hadn't looked back to see who was chasing me. I'd used alleys and backstreets and stuck to the shadows. I'd run several kilometres by midnight.

And then I had ended up here. For three months, I'd been living in hiding, paying the rent with the cash everybody had shoved into my tux at the wedding. I spent my days lying on the mattress with the window open, listening to my neighbours fighting: Wazza would steal Shazza's packet of smokes, causing Shazza to turn around and steal Wazza's. I kept to myself because I didn't want to be seen by anyone, but also because I lacked bite and energy. One day I tried joining the gym, but I saw someone from the mosque through the window. The first thing I'd done was change my SIM card and phone number.

Thus undisturbed, I lay on the mattress, searching for an epiphany.

That, and writing to Sisi.

Moe Greene had told me via email she'd been married off to a cousin. I put my heart back together by drafting and redrafting one final handwritten letter.

> Maybe, somehow, sometime, somewhere, we'll get back together. Inshallah.
> I will keep listening to the music of Usher until I die. When I listen to him, I cry. When I cry, I let out all my pain. Fuck soccer and acting. In this world I had only one person.
> I love you, forever.

There were infinite variations. None of them would do, but I was grateful: so long as I kept writing and writing, it wasn't, it couldn't be, over.

Rent was due in April, and I didn't have it. I paced all day, knowing what I had to do, but delaying the inevitable as long as possible.

Finally, I picked up the phone.

'Hello.'

'Dad?'

'Where are you?'

I gave him the address, all in one breath, and hung up the phone. I spent the day sweaty and restless and tense. I was prepared for the worst confrontation.

But when he knocked on the door, there was a box of sweets in his hand.

'How are you, son?' said my dad.

He looked around the room for somewhere to sit, and finally perched on the mattress. I stood awkwardly by the door for a second, then gingerly sat down beside him.

'I'm okay. How's Mum?' I asked. Since Mum had been the one who'd chosen Yomna for me, I knew she'd have copped it the worst.

'She just wants to see you,' Dad said simply. 'Your mother will always love you. She is upset and maybe a touch angry, but you are her son. Her first. You must come home.'

This was, I realised, what I'd wanted him to say. But I hadn't allowed myself to hope for it. I wanted to get back to work, and my studies. Possibly even real studies. I missed everyone. I missed my brothers and sisters, my mates. I missed the mosque. I missed Mum and Dad most of all. But I'd been certain that all of these treasured belongings were things I'd have to leave behind.

'I feel like you will never have the son you deserve,' I said.

Where had that come from? I felt a huge wave of endorphins relax me, like some kind of cosmic floodgate had just opened.

After all the lying and posturing and trying to please other people, it was startling to put my cards on the table.

'Then I have been a very bad father,' replied my father. 'If I have not communicated to you how much you are loved then I am the failure. I am the bad Muslim. Because you are loved without conditions. You and your insane brother Moe and the calm one Ali and your brilliant sisters. Oh, and the baby. What do you want to do with your studies?'

'I don't *know*,' I blurted. 'With our family, you're either a doctor or a cabbie. There is no middle ground. And Dad, I don't want to be either. I just want to make you proud.'

'Then be proud of yourself,' he said firmly. 'There are a million ways to serve God. I wish I'd made that clearer to you.'

I looked at the ground, then back at Dad. Outside, the neighbours were shouting and the sun was baking the hot little room.

I mustered some courage.

'How is Yomna?' I asked.

Dad looked me in the eye. 'Sad,' he said. 'What do you wish to do about her?'

I didn't know what I wished to do about her. 'I knew she wouldn't have a proper life with me,' I said, in lieu of an answer.

'Is there someone else?' Dad asked.

I stared back at him. The unsent letter to Sisi was still on the writing table. I nodded.

Dad didn't let out a sigh, or a scream, or get up and leave. He nodded back at me. 'How long have you been with her?'

I didn't answer.

'Before the engagement?'

I didn't contest it.

'*Long* before the engagement?'

'Yeah,' I mumbled.

'Osamah, why didn't you tell me?'

'Because it was hard,' I said. 'It happened too fast. And nobody would have approved of her.' He looked about to protest. 'Believe me, you wouldn't have. She's Muslim, but not like us. She doesn't wear the scarf. She was born here.'

I'd once tried raising the subject of marrying a local with Mum, but she'd said girls brought up in Australia were different. When I'd argued that God said all of us were the children of one earth, she said that was before they discovered Australia. Girls born here were like our dishwasher: when we bought it, we thought it was brand new, and later discovered it was a floor model.

'Have you contacted her?' Dad asked.

'No.'

'Maybe you should.'

I just stared at Dad.

'That is, if you're serious about her. Otherwise, what you've just told me is a story about lust, nothing more.'

'I think she's married, Dad. In Lebanon.'

'You think you know a lot of things,' he said. 'And maybe you're right. But if it is love, who knows? Maybe she's in exactly the same position as you. Although hopefully not hiding out in a building filled with the smell of marijuana.'

The thought of Sisi in a building like this made me laugh, despite myself.

'Of course,' he went on, 'assuming she *isn't* married, then I'll have to put on my mantle and turban and take you to her parents' house and ask for her hand.'

My eyes widened. 'Wait, what?'

'You heard me.'

I processed everything, but none of the maths added up in my head—unless one thing had happened without my realising it, while I was holed up in this cheap flat. 'Dad, am I divorced?'

REPENTANCE

Dad nodded sadly. 'Already, at age nineteen. But to protect Yomna's dignity, Abu Ghazi came up with a useful excuse for the annulment. Everyone at the mosque thinks you're impotent now. There's always a price.'

Dad did his best to suppress a smile, but just couldn't.

❖ ❖ ❖

Sunday, 10 March 2002, 04.18 pm
Subject: Marriage

Hi Osamah aka Da Kool Guy,
   How are you?
   First of all, thank you for your lovely ten-page email. The bit about your impotence was funny.
   You said, 'If I'm crazy enough to go to fake school for a year, then believe me when I say I'll go to the airport every day in the hope that you'll come home from Lebanon.' That was cute. You must have been going for a few days now, right? How is life at the airport? Do you get bored? Do you make the guards suspicious? Please say hi to them for me.
   So, to business. Sadly, my engagement went ahead. My wedding was scheduled for the 14th of January. But the other thing I want to tell you is that I DIDN'T GO THROUGH WITH IT EITHER. Your dad was right; maybe he's Da Kool Guy in your family. Although I didn't do your stupid thing of getting married and divorced on the same night. I called it off a week earlier.
   NOW I AM BACK IN AUSTRALIAAAAAAA!
   So IFFFFF you are interested, bring your father the cleric to our house and come convince my dad of you-know-what. He's a big Essendon supporter so maybe if you guys can get him a Bombers membership that might sweeten the deal.

Okay, get your ass over here ASAP, otherwise I'll be shipped away somewhere else. I'm in demand, baby ;)

MzLebanon
P.S. I know it's your birthday. Happy birthday. Nineteen is so old.

The time I got married again

Sisi lived in a simple house in Lilydale, tucked behind a milk bar. She had a neat room, except for the basketball trophies—you couldn't keep that many basketball trophies tidy. I didn't know why we couldn't do this in the lounge room, but whatever the case, here we were. I wore a black jacket, black pants and no tie; Sisi a simple but beautiful red dress.

Mum was chatting away happily to Sisi's mother, and that was good news. 'But the thing about Lebanese food,' she said, with a big smile on her face, 'compared to Iraq's—'

Before she could finish, Dad walked in, thank God.

He'd gone downstairs to ablute and collect the Holy Koran. He returned in full attire. We all stood up. He looked around at all of us crammed into the room: me, Sisi, her parents, my mother, her younger sisters, her two brothers too.

'I once presided over a wedding in a war bunker. This isn't too dissimilar,' he said.

He laughed, breaking the tension. We followed. We had to. We were family now.

'Before we commence with the vows, I want to thank Sisi's family for being great hosts. Who said you need a big reception to please the soul? Of course, we all would have liked something less low-key, but given the circumstances…' The entire community had witnessed my daring flight from the 7-Eleven, and while they would've shown up to any wedding I had, they were all still somewhat traumatised.

'I also want to share with you a story that is very close to me and quite meaningful in this scenario,' said my dad. 'It is about a father, his son and their donkey.'

In other words, it was parable time.

'But I know the lovebirds are eager to read the vows,' he said. 'So let's get started, shall we? We can come back later to this tale over some cake.'

MAN OF A THOUSAND SENSES

Mashhad, Iran, 2013

There is only one check-in counter open for my flight out of Iran, and between me and this counter is an incredibly long queue. There's a massive hold-up at the front, as a Saudi man in white *dishdasha* is arguing with the airport staff about his excess baggage. He is speaking Arabic; the ground staff speak back in Farsi. This is not getting them anywhere, and it happens all the time.

I look at his luggage—my goodness. You could use those suitcases to hold down enemy lines. Then I notice the Saudi man is accompanied by four wives, all in full black hijab, faces covered by the niqab. 'It's not my fault,' the man's complaining in Arabic. 'My wives went out and bought the whole city of Mashhad.'

He pleads with the Qatar rep to discount his fee. The Qatar rep shows him a calculator: it's 500 kilograms.

The man raises both arms skyward and begins to complain to God: 'Why, God? Why did you bestow upon me these women who can't do simple math!' He strikes his head with his own two palms.

Then he turns to one of the accused.

'YOU! It's you! It's all your fault!' he screams. 'What did you buy, a washing machine? YOUUUUU!'

As he drags out the final you, the angry finger still pointing, the woman under the niqab casually lifts her veil. Realising he's got the wrong wife, the man turns to the one beside her.

'It was YOUUUUU!' he fumes.

He has the right one this time, but she shoots back at him. 'Why did you marry me if you couldn't handle me?' she says. 'You should have stuck with the three bitches you've got.'

To the Iranians it's just a crazy Saudi fighting with his wives. But since I can understand it, it's much-needed pre-flight relief. I do have a connecting flight in Doha to worry about, but I've also started thinking things might work out for the best.

The women have begun to call each other names, leaving the hapless husband to do his best to intervene. 'Right,' he says. 'When we get to Saudi, you are not allowed in each other's rooms.' One of the quieter wives slowly raises her middle finger. Another simply sits on the floor.

'I'm not moving,' she says.

Only one of them moves to comfort the man. I'm assuming it's his first.

While I wait yet again, I start to ponder the odds of me leaving the country: what price would the bookies back home put on me, say, to leave Iran—$5? Leaving with Dad in tow, more like $7? And how about leaving Iran without starting a fight? Given how short my fuse is by now, they'd be up to $50 for that one.

Finally, the Saudi whips out his gold credit card. He pays millions in Iranian, the wife ends her sit-in, and the queue moves.

I check in everything except Dad's walking stick, and a small carry bag, to keep his white turban from getting crushed.

At the customs desk, the officer looks at my passport photo, then me, then back again. Finally, his gaze rests on me.

'Is this you?' he says.

I know I've lost weight, lost spirit, barely showered, grown a beard. 'Yes, sir,' I say.

'You have to get this updated.'

'As soon as I get home,' I promise.

He studies me again. 'We look at the ears, you know. That's how we know it's you.'

Thank God I haven't lost my ears. He stamps the book and moves me through.

◆ ◆ ◆

I sit in the assigned seat with my seatbelt duly buckled.

We're twenty minutes past departure time, and the plane hasn't moved.

Again, the culprit is the inept Saudi man.

I'm being uncharitable. His mother is wheelchair-bound, and Qatar can't find a wheelchair that will fit in the aisle.

That's not anyone's fault, least of all his. I feel some compassion. It isn't easy travelling with your parents—believe me, after this week, I know. They're enough of a handful to stress the calmest person out.

Just when I'm feeling a kind of brotherhood with this man, an Iranian couple informs him he's sitting in their seats. Thanks to the language barrier, this is a real problem. The Iranians are simply waving their boarding passes at him; but he just starts ignoring them after his initial 'no'. They speak to him in English; he refuses to reply.

The baggage issue was sort of funny; this situation, less so. I only have a one-hour buffer in Doha, so we're burning precious time.

One attendant—a beautiful, voluptuous Lebanese woman—speaks Arabic. She kneels at his side and asks him gently to move, and allow the Persian couple to take their assigned seats.

He turns to look at her. His eyeline crashes into her bulging breasts. He pauses, then casts his eyes down, asking her gently to move her 'self' a little to the left so they can 'converse'. Once she adjusts, the Saudi man tells her that he will not move; he wants his wives and mother sitting in the same row.

She tries again, friendly and professional and informative. 'The flight will be delayed if you can't cooperate,' she says.

The man puts on his headphones and stares at the seatback LCD screen, which is currently screening a stationary map of Iran.

I can hear the Iranians humming profanities in Farsi, some of them at the stubborn man, some just at Arabs in general.

And just like that, a troop of soldiers rushes into the cabin and demands the Saudi man move to his allocated seat.

He shoos away the soldiers. He really doesn't want to budge.

I get up, tap the Saudi man on his shoulder and let him have it. 'You are a Saudi man,' I say sternly. 'You come from the land of the Prophet. Are you telling me this is how the Prophet taught you to behave?'

He is livid at the insinuation that he hasn't been raised well. 'Would you leave your wives next to strangers?' he yells.

'Wives?' I yell. 'Why would I want wives? So I can start behaving like a dickhead on a plane?'

'I will teach you manners,' he growls, gets up from the seat, and lunges. As he barrels towards me, I grab his collar hard. I hold him stiff and close—in a locked, upright position—until a soldier yells for me to let go.

I stare at the Saudi man. He looks pathetic, and out of sorts. As soon as I release him, though, he can't help but deliver a thick, juicy slap directly to my face. My ears go *wang* and I can't hear anyone or anything. My instincts say to punch him back, but the soldiers are already edgy, and I know this would land me someplace very far from home.

The Iranian couple are muttering about this 'poor Arab display'. I turn around and surprise them by switching to Farsi, telling them they can both go to hell.

The couple look at me in surprise, then at the Saudi. 'Let's just use his seats, then,' they say, and move to the back of the plane.

The soldiers leave. The Saudi sits. He doesn't look back at me.

A couple of minutes later, the Lebanese attendant returns.

'Sorry, sir,' she whispers to the Saudi, at a kneel. 'We haven't been able to find a wheelchair thin enough. Is she able to walk in by an aide's side, by any chance?'

The Saudi man peers to the front of the flight; my eyes follow his. An old woman in a wheelchair is trapped near the door. 'She can walk,' he says, 'but she'll need two people and a frame to lean on.' The Lebanese attendant is anxious and upset. She apologises sincerely for the lack of correct facilities. The Saudi man ignores her. 'No male can touch my mother, apart from me,' he says. He recruits one of his sturdier wives to help.

And just then, I get up and tap him on the shoulder once more. He turns, hostile but uncertain. I extend my arm. He regards it. Then he seizes my dad's walking stick, gracious and somewhat startled.

My holiday in Iran has been somewhat devoid of beauty. A late exception is getting to watch an old, frail Saudi woman being led down the cabin by a man who has just slapped me, leaning on my father's cane.

❖ ❖ ❖

When the plane lands in Doha, many women take off their scarves. Some have been drinking alcohol since the plane crossed the border.

I can't believe Dad's stowed away, in the cargo hold below us.

I can't believe we've landed.

I can't believe this is all real.

I remember my first flight—from Iran to Australia. That day, Dad sat beside me, filling out his arrival card, creating strange letters in a foreign alphabet. As he embellished the card, I was gaping, and he was patiently explaining why the women were taking off their scarves, what all the bubbly drinks were. He probably noticed I was staring at the blonde, cherry-lipped flight attendant. He was the man of a thousand senses. But he'd let me watch.

The Saudi man is still in his seat, waiting for everyone to go.

As I'm fetching my small carry-on, I feel him tap my shoulder.

I turn around, thinking he wants to return my father's cane.

But his fists just fly towards me. He cups my face in both palms, pulling me towards him, and kissing me on the brow.

'You are like a son to me, and I'm sorry I lost it.'

'I'm the one who should be sorry. I should've been more diplomatic.'

He shrugs. 'I guess we were both on our last nerves. Never marry more than one wife, son. It's not as glamorous as it looks.'

I thank him for the sage advice and leave the cane with him.

Acknowledgements

This book is the culmination of the energy and love I have been surrounded by, without which I couldn't have even typed the first letter of my own name.

First and foremost, I must thank Hardie Grant for giving me the opportunity to tell my story and then for their patience, which at times was on par with Prophet Job's. Fran, my publisher, who was my first champion, and then Meelee, my editor, for humouring me even when the writing wasn't so humorous, and Ronnie and Nikki for all the hard work as we sprinted to the finish line.

I need to thank my close friends who have been extremely supportive throughout this process and have also, like my editor, laughed at my jokes even when they were flatter than a flat white.

Thank you also Salme, Kim and Asal—three young ladies who listened to my story from start to finish when I returned from Iran. Rain, thank you for your support and enthusiasm for life. Reza, the not-so-young man, thank you also.

Nicole, your love over the past decade has been honey in a hurricane. Thank you.

Shahin—you are a true mate. Your values and hope in humanity have helped me become a better man.

I thank my cousins and extended family, who live on different continents due to circumstance, for their encouragement, love and support.

ACKNOWLEDGEMENTS

I thank all my teachers, past and present, for they are the bedrock of my being.

Abbas Arezumand, the first man who introduced me to storytelling.

Michael Rowland, for opening an early door for me and remaining a friend, despite the fact that I opted out of vegetarianism.

And Tony Ayres—for all his love and incredible, delicate support. Meeting and working with Tony eventually paved the path to write this memoir and I am eternally grateful.

Andrew Knight. 'The' Andrew Knight. Thank you so much for teaching me so much. And for the heated, cool discussions on the plight of the Essendon Bombers FC.

I give thanks, a special thanks, to John Orscik for being my mentor and friend since the day I decided to dive into the creative life. Since day one. Walking into TAFTA changed my life and I will always be indebted to you.

John and Wendy, thank you for all your support throughout the years and being more than agents—friends, which are rare as yourselves.

I thank Soukena, who is not only the mother of my children but stood by me when buildings were collapsing and even went as far as shielding me from debris. The sacrifices you made will never be forgotten.

My family: you are all flowers in my heart garden. I love you all. From Mum who always found ways to fund creative classes in a war-torn country, to Moe Greene for his enormously generous heart, to Ali my true brother, to Mona and Roah my sisters, to Hassan and Hussain my little bros.

Of little ones, Sama, my young daughter—thank you for keeping me accountable and teaching me care and love. And Sara, who makes me feel alive.

And Dad. He was my confidant, friend and absolute hero.

Osamah Sami is a failed cricketer and a struggling Muslim. His choice to forge a career as an artist (actor/writer/comedian) has caused his loved ones terrible anxiety. His mother would love nothing more than for him to get real employment—at the local IGA. (If it was good enough for Anh Do, it's good enough for her son.)

He was born in war-torn Iran to Iraqi parents, and escaped to Australia with his family when he was a teen. Those experiences moulded him into a confused soul; it is a miracle he is still entrusted to write and perform.

As a writer, he has completed two feature films: *Ali's Wedding**, a Muslim romantic comedy based on the events in this book, and *Be Less Beautiful*, filming in 2016. He has also written a vague number of plays, co-created and developed the eight-episode sitcom *Baghdad to the Burbs*, and co-created the web series *2 Refugees and a Blonde*.

On stage he has performed for Belvoir St Theatre Company, Big West, La Mamma, Melbourne Theatre Company, Theatre@Risk, and in over two dozen other independent shows. Osamah also played the title role in *Saddam the Musical*, which got him deported from the U.S., having been mistaken for a terrorist. In fairness, he does barrack for AFL team the Bombers.

He played the lead role in the film *Saved* (directed by Tony Ayres), opposite Claudia Karvan, and in Dee McLachlan's award-winning *10 Terrorists!* On television, he has appeared in the shows *Kick*, *City Homicide*, *East West 101*, *Sea Patrol* and *Rush*. Contrary to popular belief, he has played a terrorist only twice.

Osamah is listed as a 'notable Australian Muslim' by the Commonwealth of Australia. He is currently investigating how this could have occurred, with one of the country's top non-Muslim private detectives emptying his bank account. He is also working on being a better father to his two beautiful daughters.

* Matchbox Pictures will release the feature film *Ali's Wedding*, starring Osamah, in 2016.